DELFGAAUW, Bernard. The Student History of Philosophy, tr. by
   N. D. Smith. Magi Books, Inc., 33 Buckingham Dr., Albany, N.Y.
   12208, 1968. 225p 68-21063. 4.95

CHOICE   JUNE '69

Philosophy

This "story of philosophy" has two outstanding merits: simplicity of
style and factual content. These two features alone make it one of the
best concise handbooks in the history of philosophy to be found anywhere. It combines an enviable wealth of information with a masterly
summary of the leading philosophical figures of the Western world.
Books of this nature, however, pose two prime problems for an author:
philosophers to be included (or excluded) and the amount of space to
be given to each. Many would most certainly disagree with Delfgaauw
in these matters. In a book of only 220 pages he includes 181 names
all the way from Thales to Newman. One wonders why De Biran, for
example, receives four and one-half pages while Darwin is disposed of
in three sentences. While many of the names will probably confuse
the beginner, he will find, however, a remarkable depth of insights into
"The Greats." The book contains neither footnotes (less serious) nor
bibliography (more serious). These minor objections aside, the book
fulfills its title and is highly recommended.

THE STUDENT HISTORY OF PHILOSOPHY

Foto Beatrix

Bernard Delfgaauw was born in Amsterdam in 1912. He studied history and philosophy at Amsterdam, Louvain, Paris and Freiburg. Since 1961 he has been professor of philosophy and dean of the faculty of philosophy at the State-University of Groningen. Dr Delfgaauw has been visiting professor at the universities of Grenoble, Genoa and Lund.

Dr Delfgaauw is the author of numerous books, of which *The Young Marx* and *Teilhard de Chardin* and *The Problem of Evolution* have been published in English. His *Twientieth-century Philosophy* will also be published shortly.

THE STUDENT HISTORY
OF PHILOSOPHY

BERNARD DELFGAAUW

Translated by

N. D. SMITH

MAGI BOOKS, INC.

33 Buckingham Drive   Albany, New York 12208

First published in English in 1968 by
M. H. Gill and Son, Limited, Dublin and Sydney,
under the title of
A Concise History of Philosophy.
Originally published as
Beknopte Geschiedenis der Wijsbegeerte
by Uitgeverij het Wereldvenster, Baarn, Holland.

First published in the United States in 1968 by Magi Books, Inc.

Printed and bound in the Republic of Ireland.

CONTENTS

3. THE FORMATION OF MODERN PHILOSOPHY

4. THE NINETEENTH CENTURY

1 Ancient Philosophy

1. *Pre-Socratic Philosophy*

European (and American) philosophy is still living from the power of Greek thought, and it is impossible to understand present-day philosophy without some knowledge of its history and its origin. In the narrower sense, this origin is Greek philosophy before Socrates. In the wider sense, it is the thought of Plato and Aristotle, and in an even wider sense, the whole of ancient thought up to the collapse of ancient civilization. This ancient thought is almost entirely a product of the Greek mind. It is difficult to establish to what extent this was influenced by eastern thought. The Romans made a relatively small number of contributions in comparison with the Greeks, and were responsible for no essentially new insights. It was not until the coming of Christianity that an entirely new element made its appearance, an element which exerted a strong influence on ancient philosophy in its final period and, what is more, brought into being a new Christian mode of thought that prepared the way, in the last centuries of the ancient world, for the philosophy of the Middle Ages.

Despite all the differences that exist between individual thinkers, western philosophy forms a unity. As Plato and Aristotle have said, this philosophy came about in the case of the Greeks as the result of wonder about what was perceived. It was an attempt to understand. The earliest philosophers were the first who were no longer satisfied with a mythical explanation and sought to find one that was rational.

As far as we know, the first Greek thinkers were inhabitants of Miletus in Ionia living in the sixth century before Christ. They are often given the name of Milesian, Ionian or early natural philosophers. The work of the Milesian natural philosophers was, however, much wider in its scope than what we nowadays mean by philosophy. For them, philosophy (the word itself is attributed to Pythagoras) was the whole sphere of rational thought, covering everything that we should now call science. It therefore included not only philosophy in the modern sense, but also mathematics, physics, astronomy, biology, medical science and politics. The division between philosophy and the special sciences came about only very gradually, mathematics being the first to follow its own course. It is, moreover, extremely difficult to say anything precise about the teaching of these early philosophers, mainly because no complete work has been preserved of any of the writers before Plato. In many cases, not even a single sentence has been handed down to us and frequently only one sentence, and we have to depend on the data that can be found in later philosophers. What has been preserved is therefore quite arbitrary and is not *a priori* reliable.

The Milesian philosophers were curious about nature rather than about man, although we should not forget that, for the Greeks, nature (*phusis*) was primarily a biological reality and only secondarily a physical reality. Their attention was directed entirely to what was externally perceptible. Even though much of what they said was to do with definite natural phenomena, the fact that they were really concerned with philosophy is clear from their search for a primordial principle (*archē*) underlying everything. This search should not be seen as a primitive form of natural science or as a disguised form of materialism. The distinction between matter and spirit had not yet been made, although these early researches certainly prepared the way for it. What preoccupied these thinkers was the need to find the primordial principle of everything, in other words, the absolute. They were the first men to look for the basis, the essential behind phenomena.

For THALES, this primordial principle was water which, in its mobility, was the living principle of all things—everything lives, as is presumably meant by the statement 'all things are full of gods'. Thales' pupil, ANAXIMANDER, called this primordial principle the indeterminate (*to apeiron*), because it had none of the qualities of the substances that are known to us. For ANAXIMENES, a generation later, the primary principle was air, which embraced the universe and was also the principle of human life, as was evident to this philosopher from the fact of breathing—'Just as our soul, which is air, holds us together, so too do breath and air encompass the universe'.

A new element was introduced by Pythagoras, a younger contemporary of Anaximenes. Two factors had an important influence on the development of Pythagoras' thought and that of his pupils. These were the Orphic mysteries with their belief in immortality and the study of mathematics. PYTHAGORAS was born on Samos, *c.* 580. He fled from Polycrates' tyranny and founded a kind of religious community at Kroton in southern Italy, dying *c.* 500 at Metapontium. It is, if anything, even more difficult to establish with any certainty the real ideas of Pythagoras than it is to establish those of the early Milesian school. Pythagoras wrote nothing himself, but merely passed on his teaching by means of oral instruction. What is more, strict secrecy was observed with regard to this teaching. The first to set it down in writing was PHILOLAUS (about the middle of the fifth century B.C.). It is therefore extremely difficult to find out what is derived from Pythagoras himself and what stems from his school.

Two points, however, appear to be established beyond doubt. The first concerns the soul, which appears for the first time in the Pythagorean school as something separate and independent, immaterial and immortal. As a punishment, it is imprisoned in the body, but it can, through purification (*katharsis*), set itself free and thus, at death, be taken up into blessedness. If this purification is insufficient, however, the soul, at death, enters another body and takes up its abode there. This is the Pythagorean doctrine of the transmigration of souls.

The second point that almost certainly goes back, at least in its original form, to Pythagoras, is the doctrine of numbers. Like the Milesians, the Pythagoreans also sought a primordial principle, and for them all things were numbers. Above all, this principle was the unit. The whole of reality was constructed from numbers, and formed an ordered whole, a cosmos. Knowledge of reality was therefore to be obtained through knowledge of numbers, and this knowledge formed an integral part of the process of purification. In this way, the Pythagoreans linked together thought and action, contemplation and behaviour.

With HERACLITUS (*c.* 535–*c.* 475), we return to Asia Minor. In all probability, this philosopher spent most of his life in Ephesus. He was between thirty and forty years younger than Anaximenes, Pythagoras and Xenophanes, and a contemporary of Parmenides. In thought, he was closely related to the early Milesian natural philosophers, but he far transcended them. He was, *par excellence*, a critical spirit. He had only scornful things to say of Pythagoras and Xenophanes, of Hesiod and even of Homer. He was himself a nobleman and full of contempt for the common people. For him, only the really great counted at all. He lived through the sacking of the Ionian cities by the Persians—only his own city in Asia Minor was spared.

Heraclitus' philosophy is that of becoming. Nothing is, everything becomes. Everything is in constant motion—'Everything passes and nothing remains'. No man can step twice into the same river, for the water is always changing. It is the same with everything. Nothing is constant, nothing is lasting. The essence of things is change and becoming. This becoming always occurs in the form of contrasts—death has its origin in life and life in death, sleep has its origin in waking and waking in sleep, age has its origin in youth and youth in age, the whole has its origin in the parts and the parts have their origin in the whole. Heraclitus thus saw the world as one great harmony in the tension of opposites, and for him too there was one primordial principle in all this. This was fire, in which everything had its origin and to which everything returned. This fire was, in Heraclitus' view, related to the spirit, so that the principle of life was also fire. This Heraclitus called the *logos*—the word, reason or meaning. Heraclitus believed that it was fitting for man to live according to the *logos*, since it was common to all men.

It is clear, then, that this philosopher also emphasized the priority of the unit. Everything is one in the *logos:* 'One has its origin in everything, and everything in one'. This unit, however, also existed for Heraclitus only in the form of contrasts. War or conflict was therefore the father of everything: 'Opposites are united and the most beautiful harmony has its origin in differences and everything comes about through conflict'. This is so not only in nature, but also in relationships between men and even in opposite tendencies in one and the same man. Heraclitus claimed to have attempted to understand himself.

From this time onwards, we are aware of a growing tendency to see the basis of everything in the one. In the case of XENOPHANES of Elea (*c.* 570–*c.* 480), this tendency is manifested in a turning away from polytheism. For him, the deity was one and everything. Monotheistic and pantheistic thought were not clearly distinguished in the philosophy of Xenophanes, who was first and foremost a poet and, in any case, strongly influenced by the religious movement of the sixth century.

The metaphysical assumptions of Xenophanes' thought were

further developed by PARMENIDES of Elea (*c.* 540–*c.* 475). Except for Heraclitus, Parmenides was undoubtedly the greatest thinker before Socrates. He seems to have been well acquainted with his predecessors and he opposed them strenuously, especially the Pythagoreans and Heraclitus. In contrast to Heraclitus' affirmation that the essence of reality was change, he affirmed the unchangeable character of being. Parmenides' great achievement was his working out of the idea of being.

He set down his thoughts in a poem bearing the customary title of *On Nature*. This poem has an introduction and two parts. In the introduction, Parmenides explains how truth was revealed to him by the deity. There are two ways of knowledge—the way of truth and the way of illusion. The way of illusion is that of sham knowledge, and this, for Parmenides, was everything that men had thought up to the present. Hitherto, he says, plurality and change have always formed the basic ideas, and both of these are founded on the illusion of the senses. Parmenides deals with this in the second part of his poem, in order, he claims, to give warning of the errors contained in this teaching.

In the first part he deals with the true reality which can only be comprehended by the intellect. Being is one, and apart from being there is only not-being which does not exist because it cannot be grasped in thought. Only being can be grasped in thought—'being and thought are the same'. And if being is one, then it can have no beginning, since it cannot proceed from nothing. It also has no end. Thus being has neither past nor future—it simply *is* in an eternal present. It is also indivisible, for, if it were divisible, there would be many beings. It is similarly unchangeable, since change includes a not-being. Finally, being extends equally far in all directions, its limit being everywhere equidistant from its centre.

It is clear therefore that Parmenides' thought was based on

a vision of genius which he tried to elaborate without ever being fully conscious of the purely spiritual character of his thought. Despite his insight into the identity of being, reality remained for him a unit in which the spiritual and the material aspects were not distinguished. As a consequence, he saw being as a sphere and thus as a material space and this resulted in his having to accept certain contradictions. His thought had to take account of the rights of the spirit as opposed to those of the senses. It was left to philosophers of a later generation to attempt a reconciliation between the two.

The later Eleatics, Zeno of Elea and Melissus of Samos, were still concerned with the problem of upholding the unity and the unchangeable character of being as distinct from sensory perceptions. ZENO attempted to show that movement was an illusion, and employed many arguments to prove this. In the best known of these arguments, he used the riddle of Achilles and the tortoise—Achilles can never overtake a tortoise because the tortoise has always advanced beyond the point where it first was at the moment that Achilles reaches this point. MELISSUS corrected the thought of Parmenides by affirming that being was infinite not only in time but also in space, thereby breaking with the Greek tradition of finite space.

Greek philosophy, however, continued to be overshadowed by Parmenides' dilemma—was reality to be found in unchangeable being or in changing phenomena? The work of the most important thinkers from Parmenides up to the time of Socrates should be considered above all within the context of this dilemma. It should, however, be borne in mind that none of these philosophers (Empedocles, Anaxagoras and Democritus) grasped the essence of Parmenides' vision and that this failure on their part was the result of the impurity of this vision, which made a hybrid unity of material and immaterial elements. As their thought is in many ways related to that of the natural philosophers of Miletus, they are sometimes known as the later natural philosophers.

EMPEDOCLES (490–435) spent most of his life in Sicily, where he was born in Agrigentum. Fragments of his poetical writings, *On Nature* and *Purifications*, have been preserved. The first is a work of natural philosophy, the second of mystical religion. The connection between them is very loose. In his book on nature, he maintained with Parmenides that in reality there was no coming into being or passing away. For him, the various forms of reality were only the result of a mingling and separation of the four elements (*rhizōmata*), water, air, fire and earth. This process is kept going by the two opposing but predominating forces of love and hatred. In the beginning, the four elements are held together in harmony by love, but hatred causes the continuous disintegration of this original harmony. Eventually, however, a counter-movement is introduced by love and the original situation is restored, whereupon the same process is repeated. Empedocles saw the origin of all living beings in this process of mingling and separation. The strangest monsters come into being, but only those beings that are capable of surviving remain in the end, in accordance with the law that similars attract and dissimilars repel each other. According to Empedocles, knowledge was a process of assimilation: 'with earth we know the earth, with water the water, with air the divine air and with fire the destroying fire'. This theory of knowledge was not materialistic, since 'everything has consciousness and shares in thought'. Finally, Empedocles taught a doctrine of the transmigration of souls in his book on the *Purifications,* similar to that of the Orphic mysteries and the Pythagoreans.

According to Aristotle, ANAXAGORAS (499–428) of Clazomenae in Asia Minor was older than Empedocles, but wrote at a later period. He was the first important philosopher to spend most of his life in Athens, where he was on friendly terms with Pericles and Euripides. After having been accused of impiety, however, he was forced to leave the city, and died at an advanced age in Lampsacus in Asia Minor.

Some fragments of his book *On Nature* have been preserved. He followed Empedocles' theory of mingling and separation, but for him the elements were not Empedocles' four basic materials or 'roots', but an infinite number of germs (*spermata*) of the most widely different properties. Anaxagoras believed that everything was formed of these particles, so that 'all things are in everything'. The most important point in his philosophy, however, was his theory of the mind or consciousness (*nous*). The *nous* caused a revolution at a definite point in the original chaos, which brought about the separation of the elements and the emergence of order. Anaxagoras was the first to express clearly the difference between mind and matter, although even he did not entirely free the mind from all its material associations: 'The *nous* is infinite and autonomous and is mingled with nothing, but is entirely by itself. It is the thinnest and the purest of all things and has perfect knowledge of all things and the greatest power. It has power over everything that has a soul, both great and small'.

Leucippus and Democritus were in line with their two predecessors. Little is known about LEUCIPPUS, but the atomist theory is attributed to him. Even in the ancient world, many believed that he never in fact existed. DEMOCRITUS (*c.* 460–370) was born at Abdera in Thrace, where he founded his school and died at a great age. Anaxagoras' theory of the smallest particles recurs in the teaching of Democritus, who called them atoms, or indivisible units. Democritus made no qualitative distinction between the atoms, but only a quantitative difference. They were, in his view, invisible and constantly in motion. This motion was possible because there was not only filled, but also empty space: 'Only the atoms and the void are real'. In this way, he gave a certain existence to nothingness: 'What is not exists just as much as what is'. It is clear from the one fragment that is attributed to Leucippus that this atomist theory resulted in a determinist view of nature: 'Nothing comes into being by chance, but everything comes into being because of necessity'. This determinism, however, is not materialism. Like Parmenides, Democritus distinguished two ways of knowing. The way of the senses was illusory, and true knowledge could only be gained by way of the intellect: 'There are two forms of knowledge, the trueborn and the bastard. To the bastard belong the following—sight, hearing, smell, taste and touch. The true-born is quite different from these. When bastard knowledge can proceed no further, because finer things have to be examined, trueborn knowledge emerges, having a finer organ with which to think'. Nonetheless, Democritus' idea of the soul remained material—for him, it consisted of the finest atoms. In his case, as in the case of his two predecessors, perception came about by the radiation of things. He was also deeply concerned with ethical problems. Happiness was, in his opinion, the goal of all conduct, but it should not be sought in transitory things: 'Happiness does not dwell in flocks or in gold; its dwelling place is the soul'. Finally, wisdom was, for Democritus, the most important virtue.

In their attempts to solve Parmenides' dilemma, the later natural philosophers undoubtedly made several important advances in thought. But they skirted the heart of the problem, which was this—how can the one of thought be reconciled with the many of perception? The solution that there were many beings, all having the character that Parmenides ascribed to being, remained a sham solution. This was perceived clearly enough by Democritus, whose answer was to give existence to nothingness. Plato and Aristotle were later to turn their minds seriously to Parmenides' dilemma, but they were able to avail themselves not only of achievements of these later natural philosophers, but also of the advances made by the Sophists and by Socrates.

2. *Socrates*

The development of Greek philosophy was so rapid that to give a short account of it in strictly chronological sequence is very difficult. The Pre-Socratics are those philosophers whose thought was not influenced by Socrates. This does not, however, necessarily mean that they preceded Socrates in time. Democritus, the Pythagorean Philolaus and the most important Sophists were of an age with Socrates; Zeno of Elea, Empedocles and Anaxagoras, on the other hand, were older contemporaries.

In his comedy, *The Clouds,* Aristophanes included Socrates among the Sophists, and this is certainly not so absurd as many scholars have later believed it to be. There are, however, many striking differences between Socrates and the Sophists. In Greek literature, the word 'sophist' had a double meaning. It could mean 'expert', and it was often used in this sense with a very favourable significance, even by Plato. At the same time, however, the word also acquired the special meaning of 'professional teacher', and in this sense it was used unfavourably. Unlike the earlier philosophers, the Sophists accepted payment for their teaching, and this lowered their status in the eyes of their compatriots. Since this paid teaching had to yield visible results, Sophism, that is 'sophistry', degenerated into a rhetorical art that was less concerned with truth than with persuasion.

This development took place gradually, although with comparative rapidity. PROTAGORAS of Abdera (*c.* 480–411) taught mainly in Athens where, like Anaxagoras, he was friendly with Pericles and Euripides. Even Plato regarded him with a certain amount of respect. His well-known saying, 'Man is the measure of all things', would seem to strike at the heart of his thinking, but it was not at all his intention to undermine every certainty. He strongly defended morals and right. It would seem that he was openly sceptical of the world of the Greek gods and was eventually obliged to leave Athens because of his views.

GORGIAS (c. 480–380) was a far more typical representative of the standard form of sophistry that became traditionally accepted in Greece. Born at Leontini in Sicily, he too enjoyed his greatest triumphs in Athens. The use of subtle technique in the art of persuasion seems to have ousted all aspiration to truth in his case, and he apparently achieved an enormous success in this, with the result that most of the outstanding younger men of Athens accepted his leadership. His most important writing, *On Nature or Not-being*, shows clearly that he advocated a complete nihilism. For Gorgias, nothing existed. Even if anything existed, we should not be able to know it, and even if we were able to know it, we should not be able to express it or communicate it.

Sophism continued further in the direction of Gorgias, but the tendency to nihilism did not prevent many fruitful studies from taking place. Logic, philology and morals owe a great debt to Sophism. The most important achievement of the Sophists was to concentrate philosophical attention entirely on man. From their time onwards, not only was nature the object of study, but above all, man himself. It would seem that it was not until the second half of the fifth century that philosophy had become mature enough to consider principally man. Certainly, by this time, it was not only the Sophists who were thinking about man, but also Democritus and Socrates.

SOCRATES (469–399) was the first philosopher to be born in Athens. He came from a very ordinary family—his father was a sculptor and his mother a midwife. He was ugly and—according to tradition—was unhappily married to Xantippe. He was a good citizen and took part in many battles. He seems to have received a good education and to have begun teaching quite early in life in Athens. Unlike the Sophists, he accepted nothing in payment for this teaching, although his association with all kinds of men provided sufficient reason for him to be regarded as a Sophist. He was interested only in man. He was, however, not concerned with persuading men, but only in making them aware of their own ideas. He was always attempting to expose sham, illusory knowledge as illusion and to go back to the real sources of knowledge. He believed that a pure intellectual insight was necessary and that this of itself led to the practice of virtue. At certain decisive moments, Socrates experienced the guidance of his *daimon*, which kept him from committing certain actions. His influence on the youth of Athens and the fact that some of his opinions deviated from those that were customarily held led to the traditional charge that he was introducing new gods and corrupting youth. He refused to leave Athens and took hemlock in 399.

It is perhaps the most difficult task in the whole history of philosophy to establish what Socrates really taught. He had a very large circle of disciples, but their writings about him differ on many points. Xenophon, Plato and Aristotle especially appear to have attempted to reproduce Socrates' own teaching, but it is unanimously agreed that Xenophon was not in a position to grasp the essence of his master's thought. Aristotle, who was born at least fifteen years after Socrates' death, could not have had first-hand information. This leaves Plato, and in his case it is particularly difficult to determine when he is reproducing Socrates' thought and when he is expressing his own ideas. Socrates must have been a man with a personality that left an indelible impression—not, like Gorgias, because of his persuasive art, but because of the true quality of his life.

It is, however, possible to summarize his thought as follows. It is man's task to care for the salvation of his soul, which is of greater value than his body. The soul is not simply man's breath, but the principle of life in a deeper sense—it is the being and essence of man as a responsible person. It is meaningless simply to live—what is important is to live well. In order to do this, man must achieve a pure understanding. If he acts wrongly, there is something lacking in his understanding. It is therefore a question of bringing man to a true understanding and insight. What is good and what is bad are not simply dependent on human caprice, but are closely related to his insight, which does not vary according to time and place, but is universally and constantly valid. Virtue is one—it is not a technique that can be taught and can be carefully adapted to circumstances, as the Sophists maintained, but possesses the unity of the pure insight.

Socrates never attempted to force a doctrine on other men. His method was that of his mother, the midwife. By questioning them, he aimed to make men understand that their current opinions were not really virtuous and contained many inner contradictions. But he did not stop at this negative stage. He continued with his questions in an attempt to bring his partners in the dialogue to a deeper understanding of the subject under discussion, which usually had some bearing on human conduct. What happened again and again in these conversations was that Socrates' partner in the dialogue would believe that he had himself come to this deeper understanding of the subject of his own accord, as a result of Socrates' questioning him. Socrates was convinced that it was only in this way that a man could make an insight really his own. This was particularly important in view of the fact that the insights were ethical ones, and therefore of radical significance to the whole of human life.

His thought continued to be felt in the so-called Socratic schools. Unlike the Pythagorean school and, later, Plato's academy, these schools were very open to other ideas. The Megarian school was founded by EUCLID (not the mathematician), one of Socrates' oldest disciples. After his master's death, he taught, in his birth-place Megara, a doctrine in which

Socratic ideas were closely associated with those of the Eleatics. This interconnection of ideas is even more evident in the later members of the Megarian school and was expressed in the Megaric philosophy by a clear preference for contradictions— the so-called eristic method (*eris,* strife). More, however, is known about the two schools which had a more far-reaching influence—the Cynical school of Antisthenes and the Cyrenaic school of Aristippus.

ANTISTHENES seems to have become a disciple of Socrates at a somewhat later age. After Socrates' death, he taught in the gymnasium called Kynosarges at Athens. This is probably the reason for the name given to his disciples—the 'Cynics'— although this name dates from a later period and may have become current partly on account of their 'dog-like' behaviour. Antisthenes was exclusively interested in ethics. In his view, man had to learn how to dissociate himself from everything and to allow nothing to cause him joy or sorrow. He had to be sufficient in himself and to see his sole aim in life in complete independence from the opinions of men and their laws. Rejecting the Greek pantheon, he put forward a monotheistic concept of God. DIOGENES of Sinope took this doctrine to its extreme limit, teaching utter contempt for man. His life is surrounded by legend (for example, his living in a barrel), but nothing can be said with any certainty about his teaching.

The views of ARISTIPPUS of Cyrene were completely opposite to those of Antisthenes. The sole end of all human activity was, in his opinion, pleasure (*hēdonē*) and, as all our perceptions are fleeting, this pleasure could only be the enjoyment of the moment. This basic proposition did not, however, exclude every form of reflection. Many factors had to be taken into consideration—for example, that much pleasure is followed by pain. Aristippus therefore maintained that the wise man never allowed himself to be ruled by pleasure but always remained its master.

The period of the Socratics is important in that it formed a link between pre-Socratic and Hellenist thought. Thus, the teaching of the Megarian school appears in one sense to be an extension of the philosophy of the Eleatics and, partly because of this, also a preparation for the later scepticism of Pyrrho. Aristippus' thought was in many ways related to that of Democritus and similarly anticipated that of Epicurus. Antisthenes' Cynical views, in which the inspiration of Heraclitus can frequently be detected, recurred in a milder form in the Stoa.

3. *Plato*

PLATO is the first Greek philosopher about whom we are relatively well informed and whose works have been completely preserved. He was born in 427 in Athens of an aristocratic family. On the fall of the Thirty, he was obliged to leave Athens and was consequently not present at Socrates' trial and death. He was apparently Socrates' disciple for eight years. He was widely travelled and acquired a great deal of knowledge in the course of his journeys. An attempt to put his theories into practice at the court of Dionysius I of Syracuse ended in failure, and he was sold as a slave. On being given his freedom, he went to Athens, where he began teaching in 387. He went back to Syracuse in 367 to make a second attempt under Dionysius II, but this also ended in failure. A final attempt in 361 also failed. Plato died in Athens in 347.

We possess all of Plato's work, at least all of it that was intended for the public. The only difficulty is in distinguishing what is authentic from what is not. A number of mainly short dialogues are certainly or extremely probably spurious. The same applies to the *Definitions*. Of the thirteen epistles, VII and VIII are in all probability genuine, and II, III, VI and XIII are presumably authentic. Opinions are divided about the dialogue

Epinomis. This leaves twenty-six dialogues which are certainly genuine. These include the great works on the *Republic* (ten books) and the *Laws* (twelve books).

It is extremely difficult to establish the chronology of these dialogues. The first attempts to do this on a basis of internal criteria were made in the nineteenth century, but such criteria can only be applied when some idea of Plato's development is already clearly established, otherwise one simply ends up in a vicious circle. The external criteria—allusions to events that are already known, linguistic style, the use of words and the use of data from other sciences—are more promising. It is possible in this way to distinguish five groups of dialogues, although even then both the sequence of the individual dialogues within each group and the boundaries between the groups themselves are often very difficult to establish beyond all doubt. The following classification may, however, be acceptable:

   I Youthful Period: *Charmides, Laches, Lysis, Euthyphro, Hippias Minor, Apology, Ion, Crito;*

  II Transition Period: *Protagoras, Gorgias, Meno, Euthydemus, Menexenus, Cratylus;*

 III Period of Ideas: *Symposium, Phaedo, Republic, Phaedrus;*

 IV Critical Period: *Theaetetus, Parmenides, Sophistes, Politicus;*

  V Period of Old Age: *Philebus, Timaeus, Critias, Laws.*

In these dialogues, Socrates is always the main person, but, as Plato became older, this Socrates tended more and more to express Plato's thoughts rather than those of the historical Socrates. As Plato's thought is an extension of Socrates', it is impossible to define exactly where Socrates ends and Plato begins. Presumably, Plato himself had no other intention throughout the whole of his life than simply to give an exposition of Socrates' thought and, where necessary, to develop it further. One of Plato's most striking characteristics is his openness of mind, his determination to make the other person think and not to force an already established doctrine on him. This, of course, is completely in the spirit of Socrates, and Plato's early dialogues, especially, very often end without any real conclusion. Plato presents Socrates here as the person who points in a certain direction, leaving his partner in the dialogue to draw his own conclusions.

It is quite evident from Plato's work that he had an intimate knowledge of his predecessors—the natural philosophers and Heraclitus, the Pythagoreans and the Eleatics and, of course, the Sophists. He treated the leading Sophists, and particularly Protagoras, with distinction. He tried to overcome the extreme antithesis between Heraclitus' denial of all rest and Parmenides' denial of all motion. This led him to develop his own doctrine of ideas without rejecting the reality of everyday experience. He was constantly striving to transcend the reality of this world but at the same time to keep a close grasp on it. The world had to be subjected to the light of ideas—Plato never saw the world as evil, but as something that man had to order. The *Republic* and the *Laws* show clearly that flight from the world was something totally alien to Plato.

His teaching also put an end to the antithesis between those philosophers who were concerned only with nature and those who were concerned only with man. Plato was concerned with both, although he was principally interested in man. His interest in man is particularly noticeable in his earlier works, but it remained predominant throughout. Like the Sophists, then, Plato was in the last resort preoccupied with man but, unlike Protagoras for example, he did not make man a law to himself, but saw him as subject to the divine laws, to the human community and to the laws of nature. According to Plato, man's task was to bring about a state of harmony—in this respect he was similar to the Pythagoreans. He resembled the philosophers of this school in another respect as well—numbers played an increasingly important part in his later works. But Plato was on his guard against the fantastic speculations of the Pythagoreans and never allowed mathematical theories to oust metaphysical ideas.

The essence of Plato's thought is to be found in his theory of ideas (forms). In this world, we perceive only changeable and transient things. How is it then possible for us to reach eternally valid knowledge? Is it not the case that what is good, true or beautiful is also always and universally good, true and beautiful for everyone? There is therefore an antithesis between the changeable, the one of Heraclitus, and the unchangeable, the one of Parmenides. But is the one bound, by the very nature of this antithesis, to exclude the other, or can the changeable and the unchangeable both exist, each at its own level? In his solution to this problem, Plato did justice both to the reality of change and to the need for eternal validity.

Perception enables us to know the changeable, but only thought enables us to know unchangeable being. The changeable is the reality of the world in which we live and which can be perceived by the senses. But the reality of this appears to be only a faulty reflection when, by thought, we reach unchangeable being. In perception, we see, for example, countless triangles that are different from each other. In thought, however, we reach the triangle as this is in itself—eternal and unchangeable. We are therefore able to perceive beautiful objects and good actions, but are able to reach beauty and goodness themselves only in our thought. Man belongs therefore both to the world of perception and to the world of thought. His task is to climb up from the world of perception to that of thought which is, in its essence, a beholding of ideas (*ideai, eidē*).

These ideas, then, are the ideas that govern our thought. They are not ideas that have to be thought out by us, but ideas that present themselves to our thought as they are in themselves, eternally and unchangeably. The reason why every man is different from every other man is that every man shares, in his own way, in the idea man. This idea is eternal and unchangeable, but it is not fully realized in any one man. This accounts both for the differences in human character and physique and for the changeable aspect of man and his mortality.

Since the things of perception share in their original ideas, perception awakens the memory of the ideas beheld before this life. This presupposes that body and soul are two distinct and separable realities. The soul has an existence of its own, but is in this life imprisoned in the body. Our striving towards knowledge in the beholding of ideas is therefore a liberating of ourselves from the body, whose passions must be controlled. The idea of the good is the highest idea of all, and all the others are known through this one. The soul which strives to behold this idea in life will also rejoice in the vision of it after death as it did even before its union with the body. Continued existence and immortality are therefore part of each other, and life on this earth is only a passing episode.

Plato, however, stressed that man is so closely bound to the world of perception that it is extremely difficult for him to ascend to the world of ideas. To do this, he has to exert great spiritual force and break all the habits of his life. Very few men are able to do this and it is made all the more difficult by the fact that the thinker is not understood by his environment and is regarded by others as a stranger who is alien to the world. The community, then, is always trying to keep man within the transient world of perception. Plato often illustrated the main points of his thought by means of a story or a myth. An example of this is his well-known myth of the cave at the beginning of the seventh book of the *Republic*, illustrating the contrast between the transient world in which man feels perfectly at home and the lasting world of ideas which can only be reached after extreme exertion.

In this underground cave are prisoners who are chained in such a way that they are only able to see the wall at the far end of the cave. A fire is burning at the entrance to the cave behind them. Between the fire and the prisoners is a low wall. Men pass along this wall, carrying various objects. All that the prisoners can see on the far wall of the cave are their own shadows and those of the objects carried past. If these prisoners have never seen anything else, how can they believe that these shadows are in any way different from the true reality?

But supposing that one of the prisoners is released and turned round so that he faces the light—would he regard what he now perceives as more true than the shadows that he saw first? Undoubtedly not, since his eyes would not be able to bear the light and he would prefer to go back into the cave. But if this prisoner is now brought out of the cave into the full light, it is obvious that the light would be too strong for him and he would see nothing. In order to make it possible for him to see the real world, it would be necessary to accustom him gradually to it. So long as this were not done, he would continue to regard the shadows as the real world.

If, on the other hand, the prisoner were gradually accustomed to the light, he would consider himself fortunate to have got to know the sun and the true reality and be sorry for his former companions who were still imprisoned. If, however, he were now to go back into the cave, he would not see so well as those who had stayed there and the others would mock him for spoiling his sight by leaving the cave and they would resist any attempts to release them.

This is also the case with man. He is so familiar with the transient world of sensory perception that he is not inclined to believe anyone who tells him that there is a reality and a truth that is higher than that of this world. If he is disposed to believe this, then he will have a very long way to go before reaching a real understanding. And once he reaches this, he will be regarded by others as a stranger who is alien to the world. Man is so certain of his perception that it is only with the greatest difficulty that he can become aware of the fact that there is a higher truth.

In his later works, Plato considered the objections that could be raised to the doctrine of ideas, in this way anticipating the difficulties that Aristotle was later to raise. His aim was to make his teaching deeper and more concrete. So long as man remained central, an increasingly important place was given to mathematics and the natural sciences. His cosmology is to be found in the *Timaeus,* a work which played a very important part in the Middle Ages. The circular movement of the heavenly bodies revealed a perfect order in the macrocosm which man, the microcosm, had to imitate in himself. Plato's two greatest works, the *Republic* and the *Laws,* show more clearly than all his other writings that his striving to reach a world transcending the senses in no way resulted in flight from the world. In both these works, Plato was anxious to give the concrete human world as ideal a form as possible, but he at no point lost sight of the fact that the perfect is unattainable and that there is consequently no question of creating the ideal state, but simply of creating as good a state as possible.

In the heyday of ancient Greek civilization, all Greeks were conscious of the intimate connection between ethics and the philosophy of the state, and Plato was no exception. For him, man's ethical duties were closely related to his citizenship, his membership of the city-state or *polis.* It was, in his view, possible to attain to full human life only through active participation in the life of the *polis.* As a result of this interconnection, a study of the state was, for Plato, at the same time a study of the ethics of the citizens of the state, which in turn led back to a study of the human soul. He saw the soul as a prisoner in the body, but he did not see it, as Aristotle did later, as a single principle, but as threefold.

The highest part of the soul is reason, which is directed towards the beholding of ideas and controls the whole of human activity if this is well ordered. The lowest part of the soul, in which the sexual and other instincts are situated, is in itself disordered and must be disciplined by reason. The rational part of the soul cannot, however, do this directly, but only with the help of the middle part, in which the higher feelings are situated—ambition, courage, just anger and so on. Reason therefore attempts to control the lower feelings by means of the higher, which it controls directly.

Plato drew conclusions from this theory which were of extreme importance educationally. Education was, for him, not simply a question of reason, but of the proper control of the higher feelings. These have to be trained in such a way that they turn spontaneously towards the reason and thus can in turn direct the lower feelings. Reason on its own is powerless. It must be supported by properly orientated higher feelings. The training of the higher feelings for this function is therefore important, and art, poetry and music play a special part in this education. In the *Phaedrus*, Plato illustrated the relationship between the three parts of the soul by the celebrated myth of the charioteer. The rational element is the charioteer himself, who drives two horses. The one horse is full of good will and represents the higher feelings. The other horse—the lower feelings—is refractory. The charioteer has to use his good horse to help him to control the bad horse—this is necessary because the chariot depends for its speed on both horses.

The virtue of justice was, in Plato's view, fundamental in the government of any state, and what was important for him was the welfare, not of those who govern the state, but of those who are governed. The rulers had to sacrifice their own interests and dedicate their whole lives to the task of government. Plato distinguished three groups in the state—the highest group being composed of the rulers, the second of warriors and the lowest group of ordinary people (agricultural workers, artisans, traders and so on). Plato demanded a great deal of those whose task it was to govern the state wisely. They were to have neither personal possessions nor a family of their own, since both could give rise to the ruler's subordination of the welfare of the state to his own interests or those of his family. This meant that the future rulers of the state had to receive a special education. Above all, they had to be philosophers, because they could govern the state only if they themselves were always orientated towards the idea of the good which, being the highest idea, shed light on all the other ideas and thus guided the rulers in their task of government.

Plato described the state in the *Laws* and in the *Republic*, but applied his teaching more strictly to the concrete situation in the former work. In both books, however, he upholds an ideal that is worth striving for, but never forgets that men are only men and that the state has consequently to take their shortcomings into account. Finally, it should be noted that Plato's state was a religious state—the state had to respect religion and its rulers had to be guided by faith in divine providence. Without this faith the state would be ruined.

Plato's philosophy is a supreme attempt to overcome the antitheses between his predecessors. He tried to avoid the dilemmas which confronted Zeno of Elea by giving the changeable and the unchangeable each its own form of reality. From the Sophists and Socrates he learnt how to see problems in the light of man's being. But it is clear that other solutions are possible apart from those which Plato saw. The question which Aristotle took as his starting-point was, which reality is in fact peculiar to the ideas. This, however, in no way diminished the lasting importance of Plato's theory of the participation (*methexis*) of everything in the world in a higher reality as a philosophical theme and the constant inspiration of his ethics.

Plato's literary legacy was carefully preserved in the Academy which he founded. Despite this, however, many later members of the Academy followed Sceptical and Eclectic tendencies. Both Plato's own work and that of his Academy were of great importance in the development of mathematics and astronomy, and it was in the Academy that philosophy was for the first time divided into logic, physics and ethics.

4. *Aristotle*

ARISTOTLE was born in 384 at Stageira in Thrace. In 367, he was sent to Athens to complete his education and was Plato's disciple there for twenty years. When Plato died in 347, he founded a school at Assos in Asia Minor under the protection of the tyrant Hermias. After this ruler had been taken prisoner by the Persians and then put to death, Aristotle went to Mitylene. In 342, however, he was invited to Pella by Philip II of Macedon to undertake the education of his son Alexander. This task did not last long, as Alexander was made co-regent in 340. In 336, when Alexander began his great campaign, Aristotle returned to Athens and founded a school there which became known as the Peripatetic school because of the habit of walking around during lessons. The disorders which broke out in Athens after Alexander's death in 323 caused Aristotle, who was accused of impiety, to flee to Euboea, where he died in the following year.

Aristotle's literary legacy raises many difficult problems. First of all, Aristotle, like Plato, wrote dialogues that were intended for the public. But these have been lost. All his surviving work is in the form of manuals of his teaching which confront us with serious problems. As handbooks, they are schematically arranged and date from various periods of Aristotle's activity. Some may even go back to the period before Plato's death while others date back to the time when he was in Assos and Pella. Most of them, however, date from the time that he was running his own school in Athens. In this school, as in Plato's Academy, the idea of individual activity together with collaboration prevailed, and this means that some of the manuals are probably the work of Aristotle's pupils, others are the result of collaboration between the teacher and his pupils and others again are simply ordinary lecture notes. Moreover, the same material is dealt with again and again, with the result that the same subjects appear in different editions, often with a fairly long interval between them. Finally, the manuscripts travelled widely before being brought together, almost three centuries later, about 50 B.C., in Rome, by Andronicus of Rhodes in a first complete edition.

Aristotle's works may be classified in the following way:

I Logical works, combined since the sixth century as the *Organon*, or 'Instrument': *Categories* (on the concept), *De interpretatione* (on judgement), *Prior Analytics* (on the syllogism), *Posterior Analytics* (on proof), *Topics* (eight books on probable proof) and *Sophistical Fallacies* (on fallacious argument, probably intended as a ninth and concluding book to the *Topics*).

II Works on natural science: *Physics* (eight books), *De Coelo* (four books), *De Generatione et Corruptione* (two books), *Meteorology* (four books), *Histories of Animals* (nine books), *De Partibus Animalium* (four books), *De Generatione Animalium* (five books), *De Motu Animalium*, *De Incessu Animalium*, *De Anima* (three books) and *Parva Naturalia* (eight smaller treatises on different subjects).

III *Metaphysics* (fourteen books), placed, in the edition already referred to, *after* the *Physics,* hence the name, which was first used by Boethius in the sixth century for the science concerned.

IV Works on 'practical' philosophy: *Eudemian Ethics* (seven books), entrusted to or edited by Aristotle's disciple, Eudemus, *Nicomachean Ethics* (ten books), entrusted to or edited by Aristotle's son, Nicomachus, *Politics* (teaching about the state in eight books), *Rhetoric* (three books) and *Poetics* (unfinished).

I shall give a very schematic outline of Aristotle's thought in the last period of his life in Athens. If his mature works are compared with what we know about his earliest dialogues, then he would seem to have developed from being a faithful disciple of Plato into an opponent of Plato's doctrine of ideas who still continued to feel himself to be Plato's disciple. Aristotle lacked his master's religious impulse, but was himself a master at the art of ordering and explaining facts. That he eventually became an obstacle to further development in science was not the fault of his enquiring spirit —except in so far as his mind reveals a tendency to regard what had once been established as proved for all time—but was due rather to the philosophical shortcomings of his later admirers, who tended to cling to what their master had said instead of conducting an independent investigation into the value of his teaching.

Aristotle's knowledge of positive science was far greater than that of Plato and he provided new insights into almost every sphere of science, especially biology. His writings show that he had made a thorough study of the works of his predecessors in philosophy and that his exposition of their propositions was quite unbiassed. His language lacks the fascination and the imagery of Plato, but he was able to express his thought with great precision. Complete agreement has still not been reached on every point in Aristotle's views. Continued research into the chronology of his works may lead to many apparent contradictions being cleared up.

Formal logic was Aristotle's creation, although the rhetoric of the Sophists and the dialectic of Plato's critical period had prepared the way for him. The central point in his logic is his doctrine of reasoning and proof. For him, reasoning took the form of the syllogism, in which two statements lead to the inference of a third. Knowledge of the nature of statements is necessary if this inference is to be correctly drawn. There are negative and affirmative, singular, particular and general statements, which can be connected in various ways. Every statement presupposes concepts and is composed of them. The statement therefore consists of the joining together or separation of two concepts (the subject and the predicate) by means of a joining or separating term (the copula with or without negation). Aristotle studied the nature of concepts and attempted to classify them in several of his works. His classification is not the same in each of the writings in which he examined concepts, but the most fully elaborated is to be found in the *Categories*. Here he listed substance (*ousia*), which relates to the essential, and nine other categories relating to the fortuitous or accidental—quantity, quality, relation, place, time, position, condition, activity and passivity. Substance is first and foremost the real, concrete thing. But different substances display essential similarities to each other, so that many substances (for example, all men) belong to the same species (i.e. man). This concept of species (*eidos*) is the Aristotelian form of the Platonic idea. Many different species may in some essential aspects be similar to each other and thus form a family or genus (*genos*). Aristotle's logic did not possess the closed character that it acquired in the case of Theophrastus and retained until as late as the nineteenth century.

It is not always easy to distinguish physics (the doctrine of material being) and metaphysics (the doctrine of being as such) in Aristotle. The point of departure for Aristotle's metaphysics was his criticism of Plato's doctrine of ideas. In this criticism, Aristotle sought to preserve both the idea as the expression of the general and the priority of the general. But what really exists in the concrete is not the general, but the particular—man does not exist, *this* man exists. This brings us face to face with two questions—how are we able, then, to speak of man in general and what is it that makes this man this man? Metaphysics and logic combine here to form a new unity. We can speak of man as such because men are similar in their essence (as a species). The differences between men are accidental and are based on matter.

Aristotle was the first to develop a philosophical concept of matter. Matter (*hulē*) was, for him, completely indeterminate. It is inherent in all finite being and is what makes the plurality of all finite beings possible. But matter cannot exist without form (*morphē, eidos*—the Platonic idea, the species of logic). Every concrete thing is composed of form and matter; it is this one concrete thing (*tode ti*) by virtue of matter and it has a definite essence (*ousia*), belongs to a definite 'species' and can therefore be known by the intellect by virtue of its form. Like Plato, Aristotle recognized two kinds of knowledge—sensory knowledge and intellectual knowledge. But both were equally real for Aristotle. Sensory knowledge grasps the concrete aspect of a definite object, intellectual knowledge grasps the essence, the species. Sensory knowledge leads to science, but is not in itself a science. Only intellectual knowledge is a science. Consequently, there was, for Aristotle as for Plato, no science of the concrete, but only of the general. In Aristotle's view, science could be reached by way of abstraction, since the intellect, which had no innate ideas of its own, could abstract its ideas, in other words, the form of things, from sensory perception.

Aristotle, claiming that he was the first to concern himself with this particular problem, also held that change was possible by virtue of matter. Only what is material can change. The relationship of matter to form is that of potentiality to act. No matter exists without form, but all matter contains the possibility, the potential of many forms, since a form can be realized in many different ways in matter. A child can grow into an adult because it is material—it can change the form of a child into that of an adult. A child is therefore a potential adult. There is thus an individual form which can always change by virtue of matter, and there is also a kind of form which expresses the unchangeable essence of things. Every essence strives to express the specific form in its individual form. This idea of finality in Aristotle's thought corresponds to the aspect of striving that is inherent in Plato's theory of ideas.

The terms potentiality (*dunamis*) and act (*energeia*) are key-words in one of Aristotle's most important philosophical themes. Two principles are present in all beings—a potential principle, or a principle of possibility, and an actualizing principle, or a principle of reality. All beings are therefore situated between two poles. On the one hand, there is the original matter, which is only a potentiality and therefore cannot really be without form and, on the other hand, there is the pure act, which contains no potentiality. (Aristotle sometimes called the deity pure actuality.) The fact that beings are formed of potentiality and act explains why they are both changeable and real. It also explains the difference between various beings of the same species—an explanation which corresponds to Plato's elucidation of this difference as the limited sharing of these beings in the same idea.

Everything that acts does so with an end in view. If that final aim for every separate being is the perfection of its own form, then, Aristotle wondered, what could be the end of the circular movement of the heavenly bodies? These were, after all, already perfect in themselves and their movement was eternal, as time is eternal. The end of their movement, Aristotle concluded, could only be a striving towards an Unmoved First Mover, who was neither in space nor outside it and was perfectly immaterial, pure form. Aristotle's First Mover moved the celestial bodies simply by means of the love that he aroused. As pure form he was also pure thought, which would not be pure if it were directed towards an object outside itself. According to Aristotle, then, the First Mover was a thinking about thought, the *nous* of Anaxagoras.

In general, Aristotle distinguished four causes (*aitia*)—the formal, the material, the final cause (i.e. the end to which a movement is directed) and the efficient cause (i.e. what brings the movement about). These causes frequently coincide—in the case of living beings, for example, their form is at the same time their end. Aristotle was not very clear about the part played by the efficient cause, possibly because he was so opposed to Democritus' mechanical view of the world.

His teaching about the soul is particularly interesting because the development of his own ideas can be clearly traced from the initial starting-point of the Platonic view, that of the dualism of soul and body. Aristotle moved away from this and, after passing through a mechanical period, became eventually convinced of the substantial unity of soul and body. The soul was, in his mature view, the form of the body and was therefore indissolubly united with it. If the soul, as the principle of life, was immortal, then the human spirit was also immortal. Aristotle was not, however, able to find a clear solution to the problem of the relationship between the soul and the spirit.

Ethics, for Aristotle, was the art by means of which man attained to the good. The good was the end towards which everything aspired in its activity. What, then, Aristotle asked, was the good peculiar to man, the good that distinguished man from all other things? His answer was the intellect. Man's ethical activity therefore attains its climax in pure thought. Man's supreme happiness is also to be found in pure thought, and every man aspires to this happiness, although he can err as regards its nature. This climax can only be attained, however, by the gods. Man, on earth, can only try to approach it by striving to keep his gaze firmly fixed on this end. In his social philosophy, Aristotle was more individualistic and more realistic than Plato. He rejected all forms of communism—man did not exist for the state, but the state was for man.

Aristotle's solution to the main questions of philosophy was different from Plato's. His mind was empirical, whereas Plato's was speculative. Philosophy is still swayed by the contrast between these two great spirits, despite the great measure of success achieved by Plotinus, Thomas Aquinas and Hegel in their attempts to achieve a reconciliation.

When Aristotle fled from Athens, he was succeeded as leader of the school by THEOPHRASTUS, who died in 287. He performed valuable work, especially in the fields of the history of philosophy, ethics and logic. But, as time passed, and others succeeded Theophrastus as leader of the Peripatetic school, interest shifted from pure philosophy to the positive sciences.

5. The Great Schools

Following the death of Aristotle, five centuries elapsed before a philosopher of equal stature appeared on the scene—Plotinus. The great schools of Epicureanism, Stoicism and Scepticism flourished during these five centuries. Many philosophers were active during this period, but they did not, like Plato and Aristotle, succeed in providing any final account of reality. The great themes were firmly established—the body, the soul, perception, thought, the will, happiness, morality and the deity; the schools of this period were mainly concerned with their correct 'dosage'. Philosophy at this time was above all something that was taught in separate subjects, such as logic, physics and ethics, and applied to the art of living. The wise man was the man who had learnt to lead his life according to reason.

As long as Greece had been independent, great emphasis had been laid, in the study of human relations, on man as a member of the *polis* or city-state. When, however, Philip of Macedon conquered the Greeks at Chaeronea (338), and the city-states lost their independence, the Greek began to feel that he was thrown back on himself. As a consequence, attention was no longer concentrated on the prosperity of the community, but on the welfare of the individual. Epicurus and the Stoics showed great wisdom and originality in their attempts to define man's attitude to life, and the Scepticism of Pyrrho and the new academy prevented philosophy from becoming too self-sufficient and dogmatic. Great care has to be exercised in our assessment of this period of philosophy too, as our information about it is generally derived from indirect sources. Only the writings of Cicero, Seneca, Marcus Aurelius and Epictetus have been more or less completely preserved.

EPICURUS was born on Samos in 341. In 306, he began teaching in Athens, where he died in 270. Epicurus' philosophy was directed to one end—that of ensuring man's happiness. Ethics consequently formed the basis of his thought, but knowledge and physics formed the necessary preparation for this. The source of all knowledge is sensory perception which, being evident in itself, gives complete certainty of the objects reached by truth. Continual perception leads to general concepts, which are as true as the perception on which they are based. Untruth can only occur in opinion or supposition, in other words, in the interpretation that we give to our perceptions. This interpretation will be true if it is confirmed by our perception, but untrue if it is in conflict with our perception. Our interpretation is, however, extremely important, because it can lead us back to the hidden principles of those things that are not immediately perceptible.

These hidden principles were, Epicurus contended, the atoms. These cannot be known by perception, but only by the intellect. Nothing has its origin in nothing and nothing becomes nothing. The universe is eternal and infinite and is formed of bodies which can be perceived and the void in which these bodies live. There is no other reality. The bodies are composed of atoms that are indivisible and unchangeable. If this were not so, things would be completely swallowed up in nothing. The only qualities that the atoms possess are form, weight and size. Their differences in form account for the different forms of various bodies and they are so small that they cannot be perceived. All atoms are in eternal movement and their main movement is a descent from above to below, caused by their weight. If this, however, were their only movement, all the atoms would fall in the same direction and this would mean that bodies could never come into existence. Bodies can only come about as the result of collision between atoms. This means that atoms must be able to change the direction of their movement for collisions to occur and bodies to come into being. Thus, the universe came about by the movement and the collision of atoms. The gods had no part either in the coming into being of the universe or in its further development.

The human soul was, in Epicurus' view, a fine body consisting of smooth, round atoms and, being essentially a body, in a position to receive impressions from other bodies. Perception was, according to Epicurus, brought about by the reception of the images sent out by these bodies, and the soul could not exist apart from the human body, with the result that continued human existence after death was impossible.

Epicurus' ethics aimed to give man serenity of soul (*ataraxia*). Fear was the foremost enemy of this serenity, fear of the anger of the gods, fear of death and fear of fate. This fear is, however, without foundation, in the first place because the gods are not concerned with the universe in which everything comes into being and occurs solely as a consequence of the movement of the atoms. The gods enjoy an eternal and imperturbable happiness of which they do not allow themselves to be deprived by concern for men. How then, Epicurus argued, can anger exist in a divine being? Men therefore have nothing to fear from the gods. Similarly, they have nothing to fear from death. The soul is mortal, which means that there can be no question of punishment in an underworld after death. Death therefore takes away all possibility of enjoyment and of suffering and is consequently neither good nor evil. We need not fear death for 'as long as we exist, there is no death and when there is death, we no longer exist'. Finally, we have no need to fear fate, since it is always possible for the atoms to change direction, thus making it possible for us to express our own free will. We are therefore not at the mercy of fate, but in control of our own actions.

All our striving is towards happiness, and this happiness will be ours if our soul is at peace and our body is healthy. It is therefore the supreme good, and all other possessions are of less importance. This does not, however, imply that we should follow every aspiration blindly. The contrary is true—we know from experience that some pleasures involve suffering and that suffering is often necessary if we are to achieve happiness. The wise man is therefore guided by his reason and regulates his aspirations. Happiness, then, is not to be found in extravagant pleasures, but in being satisfied with very little.

The affinity of Epicurus' ideas with those of Democritus on the one hand and those of Aristippus on the other is, of course, quite clear. For Democritus, the atoms had only form and size; for Epicurus, they also had weight. This accounts for their difference in movement—Democritus held that they moved in all directions, whereas Epicurus believed that they descended from above to below. But this theory compelled Epicurus to accept the possibility of a change of direction, since otherwise the atoms could never collide with each other, and he made use of this to escape from Democritus' complete determinism and to insist on the freedom of the human will. He also avoided Aristippus' theory of pleasure, in which physical pleasure and pain outweighed spiritual pleasure and pain. For him, serenity of the soul was more important than physical health, although this was also necessary to perfect happiness.

Epicurus' philosophy had a lasting influence in the ancient world, although his school produced no great thinkers, with the possible exception of the Roman poet LUCRETIUS (95–51). In his *De Rerum Natura,* Lucretius gave a faithful exposition of Epicurus' thought in poetic form, even amplifying it in certain respects with the help of Empedocles' philosophy, among others.

Unlike Epicureanism, the Stoa had a long history and continued to develop. It can be divided into three main periods— the Early Greek Stoa, the so-called Middle Stoa and the Later Roman Stoa. The founder of the school was ZENO of Citium (336–264). From 300 until the year of his death, he taught in the Painted Porch in Athens (*Stoa poikilē*), which gave its name to the school. The highest point in the second period of Stoicism (the Middle Stoa) was reached by PANAETIUS of Rhodes (180–108) and POSEIDONIUS of Apameia (135–51), who were in close contact with Roman life. In the third period, the leading figures were Romans—SENECA (3 B.C.–A.D. 65), EPICTETUS (50–138) and MARCUS AURELIUS (121–180). It would be impossible to trace the whole development of Stoic thought in a book such as this, especially as it is quite capricious and the later Stoics often end where the early Stoics began. I shall therefore only give a broad outline of the Stoic philosophy.

As in the case of Epicurus, knowledge was, for the Stoics,

based on the evidence of the senses. This in turn led to general concepts, but these did not themselves correspond to any reality. Only those objects that could be reached by the knowledge of the senses were real to the Stoics. The Stoic theory of knowledge was thus closely linked to the Stoic teaching of physics. Thus, there was no reality other than material reality. There were, however, two principles in this reality—a passive principle, or matter in the narrow sense, and an active principle, or reason, which penetrated everything. But this reason was material, an effluvium which inspired all matter. As with Heraclitus, it was fire, a fire which produced all the other elements and the whole world. Like Heraclitus, most of the Stoics believed that the world was periodically destroyed by fire (*ekpurōsis*) and rose again in exactly the same way. They also thought that the human soul was formed of this fire, but held divergent views about the continued existence of the soul.

For the Stoics, God and nature were identical, although certain Stoics had a concept of God which rejected partly if not entirely this pantheistic character in favour of monotheism. As everything was controlled by divine reason, it was also subject to the law of this reason, inexorable Fate. The world was seen as a unity in which everything was interconnected by unbreakable links of causality. Providence was the Fate that brought about this harmony. But if God was Reason, Nature, Fate or Providence, where, then, did evil come from? The Stoics claimed that all evil was merely apparent: what seems to us, from our limited point of view, to be evil is in fact good in the world as a whole. What appears to us to disrupt the harmony of the world is really an essential part of this harmony.

As in the case of Epicurus, the ethics of the Stoa were the consequence of this view of the world. Man is a part of the world and his task is to live in harmony with the harmony of the world. He does this when he lives in harmony with himself, and it is the man who lives according to reason who is in harmony with himself. Virtue is therefore right reason (*recta ratio*), in other words, reason which is in accordance with world reason. The virtuous man has therefore to control his passions and be governed in all things by reason alone, so as to live in accordance with world reason. He will also accept everything from Fate, because it is reasonable to accept what is offered by rational Fate. In this way, he can enjoy real freedom, because he desires nothing except virtue, which is the acceptance of his Fate. It is only in this way that man can find true happiness, because it is only in this way that he can realize himself. It is in this way too that he can achieve the ideal of the wise man—to live according to nature.

The wise man eliminates all feeling—his ideal is freedom from all passions (*apatheia*). Only striving towards virtue has value for the wise man, and wisdom is one of the chief virtues. It is, however, indissolubly linked with the other chief virtues of justice, temperance and courage. In contrast to these chief virtues, there are the chief Stoic faults of ignorance, injustice, intemperance and cowardice. For the Stoic, however, man was always either virtuous or bad; there was no possibility, in the philosophy of the Stoa, of both virtues and vices existing together in one and the same man. The man who values only virtue is indifferent to all the rest—honour, wealth, health and so on. This did not, however, mean that the Stoic remained aloof from social life. On the contrary, he was actively concerned with it, believing that right reason had to prevail in society as much as in the individual. Hence the value accorded in the Stoic philosophy to justice and the part played by the Stoics in society.

The Stoa combined a view of nature that was inspired by Heraclitus with a mitigated and more deeply thought-out morality which owed much to the Cynics. This did not mean that the Cynical school was completely swallowed up by the Stoa. Each continued independent of the other, although, compared with the Stoa, the Cynical school was unimportant. The Stoa exerted an exceptionally strong influence in its last period especially, when its philosophy became closely associated with the austerity of the Roman spirit. In theory, the Stoic philosophy was as materialistic as the teaching of Epicurus, but in practice it tended, like Epicurus' thought, to draw man away from the purely material and to present him with a spiritual ideal of life, tranquillity of soul (*autarkeia*). Furthermore, the Stoa was not, like Epicureanism, closed to other influences. This is quite possibly connected with its other view with regard to public life. Whereas Epicurus advised his disciples to withdraw as far as possible from all public duties, the Stoics had a strong inclination to take part in public life. Unlike most of the schools after Theophrastus, the Stoics were very interested in logic. The logic of the proposition owes its origin to them, and Chrysippus especially carried out pioneering work in this sphere.

Just as Epicureanism had links with the Cyrenaic school of Aristippus and the Stoa with the Cynicism of Antisthenes, so too would the Scepticism of PYRRHO (365–275) appear to be related to the traditional teaching of the school of Megara. Pyrrho himself wrote nothing and the tradition with regard to his teaching is very uncertain. He apparently agreed with Epicurus and Zeno, however, in trying to find the ideal of the wise man and consequently in giving a central position to human conduct in his thought. We can know nothing about things themselves and it is, for this reason, wise not to consider them. It is only in this way that we can find and preserve tranquillity of mind. Scepticism continued as one of the movements within ancient philosophy to the very end.

Eclecticism was fairly closely connected with the Sceptic philosophy. The Eclectics combined elements of various philosophies, without investigating the possibility of any inner connection between them. The Romans, who had little inclination towards philosophy, were, however, influenced by Eclecticism—CICERO (106–43) is a striking example of this.

6. Neo-Platonism

Undermined by Scepticism, the influence of the Stoics and the Epicureans diminished rapidly towards the end of the second century after Christ. Men became increasingly convinced of the failure of Greek philosophy and of the need to look elsewhere for the solution to the most urgent problems of life. The Orphic and Dionysian mysteries began to flourish again, and more and more interest was taken in oriental religions and wisdom. The increasing influence of Eclecticism made it possible for these non-Western elements to be assimilated. PHILO (25 B.C.–A.D. 50) exerted a considerable influence on Christian and on pagan thought. Living in Alexandria, the place where the eastern and western views of life were most closely in contact with each other, he tried to combine the religion of the Jews with the wisdom of the Greeks. The most important themes in his philosophy were the existence and the essence of God and God's relationship with the world.

Philo's thought was greatly influenced by that of Plato. PLOTINUS, by completely renewing Plato's philosophy, achieved even more. Born in Egypt in 204, he settled down, after travelling extensively, at the age of forty in Rome, where he found a great number of enthusiastic and dedicated disciples. After his death in 270, his writings were collected and published by his disciple Porphyry. They were divided into six groups, each consisting of nine books, and consequently given the name *Enneads*. Plotinus was the last of the great Greek philosophers, and his thought was inspired especially by Plato, although he also made considerable use of Aristotelian elements. He tried to replace the Stoic and the Epicurean ideal by a more exalted attitude to life. Even more than in the case of the

Stoics, many aspects of his thought show points of similarity with Christianity. It is, however, not clear whether he was directly influenced by Christianity or whether he wished his philosophy to act as a counterpoise to Christianity. Many difficulties are involved in interpreting Plotinus' thought. It is not always easy to make his ideas agree with each other, and this may be due largely to faults in Porphyry's text. Plotinus was not systematic in the presentation of his ideas, and Porphyry sometimes related them to each other in a fairly arbitrary manner.

In two respects, Plotinus' philosophy is different from the whole of Greek thought that preceded it—it is a philosophy of inwardness and at the same time of infinity. The Greeks regarded infinity as imperfect. Plotinus, on the other hand, regarded it as the highest perfection. Greek thought was primarily directed towards the outside world, even in the case of thinkers such as Plato and Aristotle. Was not even Plato principally concerned, in his ideas, with providing an explanation of material things? For Plotinus, only the inner experience of union with God was valid, and the entire outside world was a means to this and at the same time a constant threat.

The idea of God is at the heart of Plotinus' thought. God is the good towards which all striving tends, the good in which everything shares in so far as it is. But these are only words used to indicate God's being, which is in itself inexpressible. In God there is neither thought nor will, since thought and will presuppose a duality. Thought appears with the world-mind (*nous*), which comes from God or the One, but which is in itself no longer completely one. The mind strives to return to God, but this means that there is a difference between its thought and what he thinks. Ideas are present in the mind as mental prefigurations of things. The world-soul (*psychē*) comes from the world-mind and then strives to return to the world-mind by considering its ideas, but at the same time it brings about the multiplicity of material things which depict the ideas. The world-soul animates matter and thus guarantees the unity of all material beings, which is a unity in multiplicity. This unity in multiplicity is clear in the case of the human body, the unity of which is lost with the soul. The lowest stage of being is formed by matter, which is not a reality in itself, but can only become reality through its union with the soul. The material world is good in so far as it *is*. Evil is only the absence of good.

Just as everything proceeds in this way from God, it is man's task to lead everything back again to God. But, in this task, man is inwardly divided—he is, on the one hand, drawn towards the material and on the other by the mind. He can lose himself in the material and be completely absorbed in it, thus becoming forgetful of his own deepest being. On the other hand, by contemplating beauty in the material world, he can move to the higher consideration of ideas, which are the original image of this beauty. Man has therefore to turn away from matter as matter so as to find the idea in matter. He is able to do this because he himself is animated matter. On the one hand, his soul is what gives form to his material body. On the other hand, however, his soul is also directed towards thought, which is the activity of the human mind. Just as the soul brings the multiplicity of the human body to unity, so also does the mind bring us to an even higher unity. In thought, there is an identity between the one who thinks and what is thought, with the result that the duality between mental capacity and what is achieved by this is cancelled out. This unity, however, is not perfect, since, even though the one who thinks and what is thought are identical, what is thought is still the object of the thinking subject. Man cannot therefore find ultimate peace in thought. This peace can only be attained by transcending all thought and reaching the state where the mind becomes one with God. This, however, is an exceptional state of mind, to which the mind is raised beyond its own power to raise itself. The mind can only prepare itself for this state by purifying itself, as far as it is able, of all multiplicity and of everything that is connected with the world. Plotinus called this exceptional state of mind ecstasy.

It would certainly be wrong to call Plotinus' thought irrationalism. His intention was, on the contrary, to take thought up to the highest point that it could reach, to the summit where it acknowledged that it was incapable of going any farther. In other words, he confronted thought with the ultimate mystery. But what he regarded as mystery soon became for his disciples a capricious phantasmagoria, in which the symbolism of numbers, astrology and prophecy played a large part. Even PORPHYRY (233–304) clearly displays this tendency, although in his case it was allied to many-sided interests. His introduction to Aristotle's *Categories* was used a great deal throughout the Middle Ages in Beothius' translation. At this period, too, there was a marked increase in the part played by the pagan world's defence against Christianity. PROCLUS (410–485) revived neo-Platonism in Athens, although his form of neo-Platonism was extremely hair-splitting and retained nothing of Plotinus' original intuition.

Christian neo-Platonic thought had existed for a long time parallel to this pagan neo-Platonism, but it was entirely orientated towards theology and consequently formed a link between ancient and medieval philosophy.

7. *Greek Patristicism*

The coming of Christianity and the emergence of the new, Christian view of life placed western philosophy in an entirely new position. At first, of course, they had no contact with each other. But even in the writings of John and Paul it is possible to find certain references to Greek philosophy and, in the first centuries of Christianity, Christian thinkers were constrained to define their attitude towards the older, classical view of life. In fact, the thinkers of the patristic period, which lasted until the eighth century, adopted various positions. Some of these thinkers rejected Greek philosophy as a purely human view of life which, since the Christian revelation, had become not only superfluous, but even dangerous. Others, however, regarded the development of Greek thought as a preparation for the gospel. Both these tendencies can be found in Greek and in Latin patristicism and they persisted until the Middle Ages.

Christian philosophy can be said to begin with JUSTIN, who was born of pagan parents in Palestine (c. 100). After a long period spent in moving from one system of Greek philosophy to another, he became a Christian in 133 and died (c. 165) as a martyr. Justin was always extremely open to Greek thought and regarded the Christian revelation as the culmination of Greek, and especially of Platonic philosophy. This attitude led to his historical statement: 'Every true thing that has ever been said comes from us Christians'. The same Logos, Justin believed, enlightened both the ancient philosopher who was seeking God and the believer in Christ—Socrates could therefore also be regarded as a witness to Christ. This formed the point of departure for a theme which was taken up by such Christian thinkers as Augustine and continued to play a very important part throughout the Middle Ages. This is also, in a sense, true of Justin's idea (which, however, goes back to the Jewish historian Flavius Josephus and to Philo of Alexandria) that the Greek philosophers derived certain of their ideas from the Bible.

The Christian philosophical concept of creation is also to be found in Justin's writings, that is, the concept of God as the Creator or maker from nothing as distinct from the Platonic concept of God as the maker of beings from an already existing matter. In fact, HERMAS had already anticipated Justin by about ten years, when he said in his *Shepherd:* 'First of all you must believe that there is one God who has established, ordered and made everything from nothing and who embraces everything but is himself incapable of being grasped'. Justin set down his thoughts in various works, of which his two *Apologies* and his *Dialogue with Trypho* have been preserved. The *Apologies* form an exposition of Christian as distinct from pagan thought; the *Dialogue* presents the Christian argument as against the Jewish.

But, as I have already noted, there was, from the very beginning, a movement in patristic thought which presented a complete contrast to Justin's attitude in its absolute rejection of Greek philosophy. Oddly enough, the first representative of this movement in literature was the Syrian TATIAN, who, like Justin, was born of pagan parents and, after a long period of study in philosophy, became a Christian. In Rome, he was a disciple of Justin's, but later he returned to the East and became a Gnostic. Despite the similarity of his life to that of Justin, and despite Justin's teaching, he took sides against the whole of Greek civilization and philosophy in his *Address to the Greeks*. At the same time, however, he did not repudiate his philosophical education in his own speculations, showing himself always, in his thinking about God, as a disciple of Justin's. He could, however, express himself far more vigorously than his master. Paul's idea of our natural knowledge of God (*Rom.* 1:19–20) was, for example, elaborated by Tatian in the following way: 'We know God from his creation and we comprehend his invisible power from his works'. This too formed the point of departure for an important theme in later thought.

An extremely important step in the tradition of Justin was made by the Athenian ATHENAGORAS in his *Plea for the Christians,* written about the year 177 and addressed to the

Emperor Marcus Aurelius. Athenagoras was very favourably disposed towards Greek philosophy, believing that it could help to elucidate and explain revealed truth. He was also convinced that natural thought could demonstrate the unity of God. He also wrote a very remarkable treatise *On the Resurrection*, in which he made, for the first time, the important distinction—a distinction which was to be decisive in all later apologetics—between the potentiality of the truth concerned and its existence as a fact. He was the first to demonstrate that man, as a rational being, has an eternal destiny. Since man is both soul and body, the soul alone cannot attain to this eternal destiny. Consequently, the moral order also requires a recompense in the life after death in which both the soul and the body must share. Finally, man's destiny is happiness, which cannot be found fully in this life. Athenagoras' view of man as a unity, that is, as consisting not of soul or of body, but of both together, is extremely important.

It is necessary to say something at this point about the Gnostics, as they recur constantly in the patristic writings. The so-called *gnōsis* (knowledge) was fundamentally a fusion of ideas taken from Greek philosophy and elements derived from the Greek mysteries on the one hand and eastern mythical notions and biblical ideas on the other. It occurred in many different forms and was later to be disputed by Augustine in the form of Manichœism. All these forms, however, have certain features in common. In the first place, the Gnostics held that there was a complete antithesis between spirit as the principle of good and matter as the principle of evil. Then they attributed the creation of the world not to God, but to lower beings of a spiritual nature. Finally, they confined redemption to the small number of those who were able to raise themselves from the level of faith to that of knowledge. Despite the high esteem in which they held knowledge, the Gnostics are of little philosophical significance because of their uncritical mingling of philosophical, mythical and biblical elements and the fact that fantasy played a more important part in their teaching than thought. This is very clearly revealed in the Gnostic document, *The Wisdom of Faith*. Apart from this writing, our knowledge of the Gnostics has been confined to quotations made by those who opposed them, such as, for example, Clement and Origen, the leaders of the Catechetical school of Alexandria. These writers continued the tradition of Justin in Christian thought and devoted themselves to the task of upholding the true knowledge of faith as opposed to the false knowledge of the Gnostics. In recent years, a large number of Gnostic manuscripts have been discovered, and this is bound to lead to a great increase in our knowledge of the essence and form of Gnosticism.

CLEMENT was probably born in Athens *c.* 150 and was, for several years around the turn of the century, the leader of the Catechetical school of Alexandria, being forced eventually to flee during Septimius Severus' persecution of the Christians. He died in Asia Minor in 215. He intended to write a trilogy forming an initiation into Christian doctrine and did in fact complete the first two parts of this work—*Protrepticus,* an inducement to embrace Christianity, and *Paedagogus,* the formation of the Christian. He did not, however, succeed in writing the third part, *Didascalus,* which was to have described Christian perfection. Another work, *Hypotyposes* (outlines) has been lost, but the notes which Clement made for *Strōmata,* which presumably contain a good deal of preparatory material for the *Didascalus,* have been preserved.

Clement had a twofold aim—on the one hand, he wished to mark Christian teaching off clearly from Greek philosophy and Gnosticism, and on the other hand to throw light on it with the help of Greek thought. He held philosophy in very high esteem, regarding it as having, in a certain sense, the same value for pagans as the law had for the Jews. This was, in his opinion, possible because it was to a very great extent based on derivation from the Bible. For the Christian, however, the starting-point of all thought was faith, although this did not render philosophy superfluous. It could, in the case of an out-sider, prepare the way for faith. In the same way, it could, for the Christian, be a means of defending his faith and of thinking it out. In Clement's view, faith (*pistis*) was the distinguishing mark of all Christians, but knowledge (*gnōsis*), which did not make faith unnecessary, but illuminated it, was higher. Whoever succeeded in living according to knowledge—the true *gnostic*—would kill his passions and, Clement taught, turn to God in a love that was purified of all passion. This concept of knowledge constituted an attack on Clement's part against the so-called Gnostics, since knowledge did not, in his view, make faith superfluous, but presupposed it. Unlike the Gnostics, he placed great emphasis on free will and man's personal respon-sibility for sin. Philosophy could in itself lead to knowledge of God, since it could, in his opinion, reach God as the cause of being in all things: 'There is nothing to which God does not impart being'. Whereas Clement's moral teaching was clearly influenced by the Stoa, there is evidence here of the large part played by Plato's philosophy. Like Philo before him, Clement accepted a double creation—the creation first of the invisible world and then of the visible world, modelled on the invisible. This idea was to be elaborated more fully later and to reach its culmination in Augustine.

ORIGEN was born in Alexandria in 185 and succeeded Clement when he was still very young as the leader of the Catechetical school. He remained in charge of the school until 231, when he founded and ran a similar school in Caesarea, where he died in 254. Origen's edition of and commentaries on the Bible formed a very large part of his work. As far as his theological and philosophical views are concerned, however, his most important works are *Against Celsus* (the Platonic philosopher who had attacked Christianity) and especially *De principiis* (*On Principles*), the first systematic exposition of theology. Creation is eternal and, from eternity, the Son proceeds from the Father and the holy Spirit is, in a manner of speaking, subordinate to both. The spirits were also created by God. These, however, were unfaithful to God and were punished by being imprisoned in bodies. The whole of visible creation, consisting of angels, men and devils, is therefore the result of sin. These creatures are all put to the test and can eventually return to God, if not after one life, then after several or even many lives. Then the complete restoration to the original state of creation (*apokatastasis*) takes place. Platonic influences are clearly discernible in this dualism of soul and body with its underrating of the body and in Origen's doctrine of the transmigration of the soul. Here, Origen's thought marked a retrogression on that of Athenagoras. His view of human free will, by which man can accept grace and thus be redeemed by Christ and led to perfection, is, however Christian. Although matter is present as a consequence of sin, it is not the cause of sin—the only cause of sin is man's free will. Origen was undeniably very close to the Gnostics in his dualism and his belief in the transmigration of the soul, but in this very important point he was diametrically opposed to them. One final point in Origen's teaching should be mentioned—his placing of the Son, the Logos, below God the Father. The invisible world was created by God, whereas the visible world was called into existence by the Logos according to the ideas which he had in him.

The three great Church Fathers of Cappadocia—Basil the Great, his younger brother Gregory of Nyssa and their mutual friend Gregory Nazianzen—occupy a very remarkable place in Greek patristicism. Although both Basil and Gregory Nazianzen contributed a great deal to the further development of philosophy, Gregory of Nyssa was, of the three, the most important philosopher. GREGORY NAZIANZEN (330–390), the Patriarch of Constantinople, developed further a theme that had already been discussed by Justin—that of our natural knowledge of God—in the second of his five *Theological Orations*. Human reason enables us to comprehend the existence of God from his creation, but not his being, about which we can only make negative statements, such as incorporeal, unbegotten, without beginning, unchangeable or not transient. The concept of creation was further developed by BASIL (330–379), the Bishop of Caesarea and the founder of eastern monasticism, in his *Six Days of Creation* (*Hexaemeron*). Only God is without beginning; the world had a beginning, and the beginning of the world was at the same time the beginning of time. World and time are thus correlated, but God's act of creation of the world was outside time.

GREGORY OF NYSSA (335–94), the Bishop of Nyssa, who was the most important of these three Fathers from the point of view of pure philosophy, was closely related to Origen in his thinking, but he attempted to prevent Christian truth from being sacrificed to Platonic speculation, as had happened frequently in the case of Origen. The influence of neo-Platonism is, however, clearly discernible in Gregory's thought. His philosophical ideas are most clearly revealed in his *Great Educational Treatise*, his book *De hominibus opificio* (*On the Making of Man*) and his dialogue *De anima et resurrectione* (*On the Soul and Resurrection*).

One of Gregory's great achievements was to distinguish between faith and knowledge. Truths which are revealed by God, but which are not understood in themselves are accepted in faith, whereas truths which are understood by knowledge are discovered by this knowledge. Knowledge can, however, be of service in the defence of the truths of faith, in the further elaboration of these truths and in the establishment of a mutual connection between them. Gregory was strenuously opposed to the neo-Platonic belittlement of matter. Matter and the body are not in themselves bad—sin is only present in man's free will. Evil has no reality of its own—it is only the absence of good. It is therefore man's task to turn his soul towards this good, in other words, towards the contemplation of God. The soul is created by God as an immaterial and rational being at the same time as the body and forms a unity with it. Although the soul has vegetative, sensitive and rational functions, it is nonetheless one and there can be no question of one body having more than one soul. There is thus no question of the pre-existence of the soul, as Origen taught, or of its transmigration —after the resurrection, both the glorified soul and the glorified body share in eternal happiness. This, however, is only possible by virtue of the grace of Christ's redemption. Although a natural knowledge of God, derived from visible creation, is possible, faith is necessary for this eternal happiness resulting from the grace of redemption. The climax of our knowledge of God is the vision of God himself.

The writings which became widely known in the sixth century as the works of DIONYSIUS, whom Paul converted on the Areopagus, exerted a very great influence on the philosophy of the Middle Ages. It has, however, since been established beyond doubt that these works originated only at the end of the fifth century. The writings of the Pseudo-Dionysius include four fairly extensive works—*De divinis nominibus* (*The Divine Names*), *De mystica theologia* (*The Mystical Theology*), *De coelesti hierarchia* (*The Celestial Hierarchy*) and *De ecclesiastica hierarchia* (*The Ecclesiastical Hierarchy*)—and ten epistles. In these works, the writer outlines Christian theology in a very original way, and his arguments reveal his knowledge of the theology of his own period and his familiarity with neo-Platonism.

God, he tells us, is the completely transcendental cause of everything that is. It is impossible to conceive him properly in thought and, as a consequence of this, to give him a proper name. He is above everything that can be conceived in thought or named and is even above being itself. But everything that proceeds from him strives to return to him, and in this striving we somehow try to conceive God in thought and to name him. In our attempts to do this, we can follow three complementary ways. In the first place, we can positively ascribe to God all that we find in the cosmos that is really good. This is the positive way. Then we can deny that all this is in God as it is in the cosmos. This is the negative way. Finally, we can affirm that all perfections are present in God in such a way that they infinitely and therefore incomprehensibly surpass all created perfections. This is the surpassing way. In this striving towards God, which constitutes the meaning of life, God bears man up by the light of his grace which shines through the whole of the cosmos. God is light, but we are too weak to perceive this light, with the consequence that, for us, it is darkness. We can, however, somehow accustom our eyes to this light and thereby gain some knowledge of God in the ways described. It is, however, not simply a matter of thought, but also of detachment from the things of this world. The divine light and human free will combine to enable man to ascend in the loving contemplation of God and to help others in this ascent. The Pseudo-Dionysius, like Gregory of Nyssa, rejected the transmigration of the soul and did not identify the body and sin and, also like him, placed great emphasis on man's free will and on evil as the absence of good.

It is possible to regard the Greek patristic period as ending with the work of JOHN DAMASCENE (d. 749). He summarized the whole of Greek patristic thought in his *Fount of Wisdom* and this book provided the medieval scholastics with an important source of information about Greek patristic philosophy and theology, the traditions of which were continued throughout the Middle Ages by the Byzantine philosophers.

8. *Latin Patristicism*

As in Greek patristicism, there were from the very beginning, two distinct attitudes towards philosophy in Latin patristicism. One school of thought rejected philosophy, whereas the other accepted it. Space does not permit me to mention any but the most important thinkers here.

TERTULLIAN (160-222) was one of those who rejected philosophy. He was born of pagan parents in Carthage, but was converted to Christianity in Rome. Round about the year 195, he returned to Carthage and at once became extremely active there as a theologian and a defender of the Christian faith. In 205 or thereabouts, his extreme rigorism impelled him to become a Montanist and he played an important part in developing the teaching of this heresy. Most of his writings, however, date from his orthodox period, although even at this time his rigorism was clearly perceptible.

In his view, the Christian revelation replaced philosophy, which could only confuse the Christian or even lead him into error. Everything that the philosophers had ever said was, according to Tertullian, unimportant in the light of revelation —the philosophers had, without acknowledging it, taken everything that was good in their teaching from the Bible. This does not, however, imply that Tertullian rejected rational thought. He recognized its value, but was apparently of the opinion that philosophy did not strengthen rational thought, but rather perverted it. He did not therefore reject rational thought about God's existence and perfection entirely. Reason could, in his view, comprehend both the existence of God and the immortality of the soul. There is also a remarkable materialistic element in Tertullian's philosophical thought and this is undoubtedly due to the fact that he was unconsciously influenced by the Stoics, whose teaching he rejected. Both God and the soul were, in his opinion, corporeal, although their bodies were of a very special nature—God, for example, being 'a body, although he is a spirit'. The soul was not created separately each time by God, but was transmitted by the parents to the child.

By far the most important and deeply influential of all the Latin Fathers was AURELIUS AUGUSTINE (354–430). After many years of searching in various philosophical schools and a period during which he was a member of the Manichæan sect, he was baptized in the Catholic Church (387). He was ordained priest in 392 and, four years later, was elected Bishop of Hippo, a diocese to the west of Carthage, where he devoted himself to pastoral work, combatted various heresies and was incessantly active as a writer. All Augustine's writings date from after his conversion. They can be divided into two periods. His writings from the time before he became a priest show him as one who was seeking for harmony between faith and philosophy. In these writings, it is frequently the philosophical element that predominates, without ever conflicting with faith. His favourite form during this period was that of the dialogue. After his ordination, however, he devoted himself mainly to the task of setting out the Church's teaching on faith. In these later writings, the philosophical element was in the background, although it remained extremely important. These works were often written over a very long period. Among those which should be mentioned here are the *Confessiones* (*The Confessions*), *De Trinitate* (*The Trinity*), and *De Civitate Dei* (*The City of God*). In his *Retractationes* (*Revisions*, 426–427), Augustine reviewed the whole of his work at the end of his life.

It is difficult to come to a really precise understanding of Augustine's philosophical thought. This is not only because he, like almost all early Christian writers, was first and foremost a theologian, but also because his writings were almost always dictated by the demands of the moment and he expressed his inner life in them in a very special way. His work was always a personal confession, in which fresh questions were constantly brought to light or the same questions were shown up in a different light. Furthermore, his thought reveals a growth which is less of a change than a penetration to a deeper level. This is clearly discernible in the *Retractationes*, which he wrote in his old age.

Augustine was convinced that all thought was meaningless if it was not capable of overcoming scepticism. Scepticism, however, is founded on an inner contradiction. Who doubts cannot doubt that he doubts. Who doubts thinks. Who thinks exists. Augustine was thus able to link the order of knowing and the order of being and to maintain that it was meaningful to aspire to truth. By thinking we come to truth and certainty, and our thought is expressed in eternal, necessary and unchangeable judgements. But this impels us to go further, for how can our thought, which is in itself contingent, come to such judgements? The existence of these judgements can only be explained from the existence of an eternal, necessary and unchangeable reality, which transcends human thought. This reality must be spiritual and personal, the source of all life and all thought. This reality is therefore the God of creation, God himself. In this way, Augustine discovered the existence of God from an analysis of human thought. This brings us to two great themes in Augustine's thought in their mutual connection —'Let me know myself, let me know thee'.

What is man? He is a very special being in the created world—according to his body, he belongs to material nature, but according to his soul, to the world of the spirit. His body and his soul are united in an original synthesis. Man belongs to the material world—he is subject to the limitations of material nature, to change, to suffering, to time. But he also belongs to the spiritual world—his intelligence seeks eternal truth, his will perfect goodness. This is the reason for the presence of conflicts in man, in which his free will has to try to subject his material inclinations to his spiritual inclinations.

This does not mean that the material is in itself bad. Sin is present only in man's free will, when he chooses to give preference to the material rather than to the spiritual, thereby making his ascent to God impossible. For Augustine, then, evil is only to be found in the absence of good.

The beginning of knowledge is sensory perception. In this perception, however, it is the soul which perceives. The intellect judges these sensory impressions and accordingly regulates human activity. In this thinking activity, however, man becomes aware of eternal, necessary and unchangeable truths, which ultimately govern all activity. Reason is the contemplation of these eternal truths which the soul perceives in itself. As I have already said, only the God of creation can explain the presence of these truths in the soul. God creates these truths, which govern thought and action, in the spirit of man. Whenever I think or act, I perceive these truths in my memory—they are an innate illumination of the human spirit.

It is clear, then, that Augustine stressed the sublimity of the human soul, each soul being united in a unique manner with its body. Eternal existence and the transmigration of the soul were for him out of the question. He maintained that the soul originated at the same time as the body, but that it did not pass away with the body because it was immortal. How, he argued, could the soul pass away, when it had in itself the possibility of contemplating the eternal truths? On the other hand, however, he was never able to decide whether he ought to accept that the soul was passed on, as Tertullian taught, by the parents to the child, or that it was separately created each time by God.

Augustine did not, however, see man simply as an individual. Man lives in a society, in which everyone is connected with everyone else by numerous bonds. These bonds are terrestrial or heavenly in nature. Thus the terrestrial state is contrasted with the heavenly state of God, in which all men are connected by love for God and in which every man's personal progress in love for God is at the same time a progress in love for the whole community.

Augustine's philosophy was a philosophy of participation— a Platonism of a very distinctive kind. By his knowledge of the eternal truths, which are fixed in his memory and made conscious by knowing, man has a share in the ideas that were in the mind of God at the creation of the world. Creation as such is a participation in the divine ideas but, in man, this participation is not simply a passive presence, but an active possibility which is capable of realization in loving knowledge, in which man may rise, by way of creation, to a loving recognition of God. This participation is, in a certain sense, brought about by knowing, but all knowing is governed by love. Thus, in Augustine's philosophy, thought and love are harmoniously and indissolubly connected. All knowing is a participation in God's will. All loving is a participation in God's goodness. All being is a participation in God's being. God's being is therefore immanent in the whole of creation, although it is at the same time transcendent to this creation. God is being as such, a being that is personal. As a person, this being produces the whole of the cosmos by free creative activity and not, as Plotinus maintained, by necessary emanation.

Augustine and the Pseudo-Dionysius exerted a greater influence on medieval thought than any of the other Church Fathers. Of the two, Augustine undoubtedly had the deeper influence and it is his thought which strikes us today as the most rewarding.

The work of BOETHIUS (480–525) played a very important part in the emergence of scholasticism. He occupied an important position in the court of King Theodoric, but fell into disfavour and was beheaded. His great contribution to the history of philosophy was his translation of many of the works of Aristotle and his commentaries on these works. Much of his translation and interpretation of Aristotle's *Organon* and his translation of Porphyry's *Introduction to the Categories* have been preserved. In addition, Boethius also wrote a number of works on logic and theological treatises and, while he was in prison, he wrote his famous book on *The Consolation of Philosophy*, which is remarkable in that it contains very few traces of Christian thought. In it, Boethius tries to find the strength to face death in philosophy alone, although it is difficult to see why he chose to restrict himself purely to philosophy, since his faith in Christianity, as illustrated in his theological writings, can hardly be regarded as open to doubt.

Patristic philosophy is essentially ancient philosophy which has passed through Christianity. As a consequence, philosophy is almost always subordinate to theology in patristic thought. It was contemporaneous with Hellenistic philosophy. The Pseudo-Dionysius, for example, was a contemporary of Proclus, and Augustine was already dead when Proclus began his work. The neo-Platonic school continued in Athens until 529, when it was closed by the Emperor Justinian four years after Boethius' death.

2 Medieval Philosophy

1. *The Emergence of Scholasticism*

Medieval scholasticism followed a different direction in philosophy from ancient thought and, in this, stands out clearly as the product both of a new age and of a different group of people, namely western European.

Medieval philosophy is often seen as too uniform and furthermore as without importance in the history of philosophy. But anyone who wishes to understand the development of philosophical thought must carefully reconsider this attitude. It is impossible to understand what happened in the Renaissance and the seventeenth century if the medieval prelude to this period of philosophy is neglected. And here I should point out that this book is a short history of *philosophical* thought, which means that theological thought must inevitably be kept in the background. The reader should therefore bear in mind that the following outline of medieval thought, which was primarily directed towards theology, is presented in a consciously one-sided way.

The barbarian invasions which brought about the downfall of the western Roman Empire, at the same time destroyed the Christian civilization that was flourishing in southern Europe and North Africa. It was impossible for any new civilization to develop in the chaotic situation that prevailed in the sixth and seventh centuries and it was only when a certain degree of political peace had been re-established in western Europe under

C

Charlemagne that scientific and artistic life could be revived. This Carolingian Renaissance was actively encouraged by the emperor himself and, in addition to science and art, philosophy also experienced a revival. This was studied especially under the heading of logic (dialectic) which, together with grammar and rhetoric, formed the *trivium*. These were the three subjects of 'primary education' and were a preparation for the *quadrivium* of arithmetic, geometry, astronomy and music which, as scientific subjects, enjoyed a greater prestige. Over the centuries, however, this emphasis gradually changed, as philosophy came to be studied, not simply within the limited framework of logic, but also in connection with the problems of the theory of knowledge, psychology and metaphysics. In addition, grammar and rhetoric were soon approached in a philosophical spirit and later on the subjects of the *quadrivium* were also studied philosophically. In the twelfth century, all seven of the *artes liberales* were taught in the schools and, among them, philosophy (dialectic) was the most important.

Philosophy was studied, as I have said, in the schools. The ancient learning was handed down in the sixth and seventh centuries by the monks, who copied the classical writings. In the more peaceful times that followed, they established schools in their monasteries where they taught either the subjects of the *trivium* or the seven subjects of the liberal arts. The bishops often followed their example and established chapter schools. The original meaning of 'scholasticism', then, was simple 'school instruction' .The word gained its adverse connotation because of the attacks of the humanists who actively engaged in battle with a scholastic thought that had fallen into disrepute in the later Middle Ages.

The monastic schools had already reached a certain point of growth in the Carolingian period, and this development was actively encouraged by Charlemagne's founding of his Palatine school, to which he summoned the most celebrated scholars of

his day. This marks the emergence of Europeanism, a movement which characterizes the whole of the Middle Ages.
Irishmen, Englishmen and Scots, Frenchmen, Germans and
Dutchmen, Italians and Spaniards travelled at this time all over
Europe and taught in the places where their learning was most
appreciated. From 781 until 796, Charlemagne's school was
under the leadership of ALCUIN (735-804), who, when he left
the Palatine school, founded the famous monastic school of
Tours. This English monk was convinced of the importance of
the liberal arts which he regarded as indispensable to the fruitful
study of Scripture. He played a particularly important part in
organizing education in the early Middle Ages.

Alcuin's thought was strongly neo-Platonic in character. This
is most apparent in his dualistic view of the relationship between
the soul and the body, which he regarded as being united more
or less by chance. This neo-Platonism typified scholastic
thought until the thirteenth century, when there was a gradual
mingling of neo-Platonic and Aristotelian elements, a very slow
process which eventually led to the emergence of a new and
original philosophy. This development was in the main the
outcome of increasing familiarity with the philosophy of the
ancient world. The first scholastics had little more than the
works of Augustine and Boethius and a translation of Plato's
Timaeus at their disposal. Thus they knew Plato only in one
dialogue, Aristotle only through the part of the *Organon*
translated by Boethius and Plotinus only through the work of
Augustine. In addition, Porphyry's *Introduction to Aristotle's
Categories*, in Boethius' translation, also had an important
influence at this time. These works formed the point of
departure for early scholastic thought, which consequently had,
via Augustine, a neo-Platonic character though such neo-
Platonism was radically changed under the influence of
Christianity, as happened in the case of Augustine's thought,
and later on also under the influence of Aristotle.

The initial impulse provided by Alcuin set medieval philosophy and theological thought in motion, but political and social unrest at the time and incomplete knowledge of ancient thought prevented them from flourishing. Their progress was undeniable but very slow, and the sudden appearance of JOHN SCOTUS ERIUGENA is therefore all the more remarkable. It is indeed still very difficult to understand how this mysterious figure could have emerged with a carefully constructed philosophical system at a time when thinkers were still working very eclectically and how he was able to know such excellent Greek in an environment in which the ancient language was still more or less entirely unknown. He was born in Ireland in about 810 and, from 847 onwards, taught at the Palatine school of Charles the Bald, who had continued the traditions of Charlemagne. In spite of ecclesiastical objections, he was allowed to stay at the court until 870, after which time it is not known what happened to him. He wrote an early work on predestination and later undertook the translation of the works of the Pseudo-Dionysius. This translation was very influential throughout the whole of the Middle Ages.

This influence is discernible in John's own writings, and especially in his *De divisione naturae*. By nature, John meant the whole of reality. Four forms can be distinguished in this total reality. The first nature is the nature that creates and is itself uncreated. This is the perfectly one nature of God, who transcends both spirit and matter and is completely incomprehensible. It is from this unity that the second nature proceeds, the nature that creates and is itself also created. This is the Logos, in whom all essences are present in a spiritual manner. The realization of these essences in the perceptible world is the third nature, the nature which is created and does not itself create. This emanation from God is followed by a return to God. As the ultimate goal of this return, God is the fourth nature, the nature which does not create and is not created. This metaphysical train of thought implies an ethic. Man must aspire to become one with God, who can only be attained in a mystical intuition which transcends both the activity of discursive reasoning and that of sensory experience.

John's translation of the works of Dionysius the Areopagite strengthened the influence of neo-Platonic thought throughout the Middle Ages. During the whole of this period, the Pseudo-Dionysius was regarded as possessing almost as much authority as Augustine. John's own thought, however, did not exert a very great influence. The pantheistic tendency of his work made it suspect in the eyes of orthodox thinkers and his thought was also far too great in its scope for his contemporaries and the thinkers of the generations which immediately followed him to be able to assimilate it properly. John Scotus Eriugena stands out as an isolated figure whose wonderful power of thought was far in advance of his time.

Science developed only very slowly in this turbulent period. Various thinkers kept alive an interest in ancient literature, in philosophy and in theology. The seven liberal arts and theology, which was mainly scriptural exegesis, were practised in close relationship with each other. A gradual change, however, came about in the eleventh century. The claims of a developing dialectic began to be strongly felt and rationalist tendencies towards a fully dialectic explanation of the mysteries of the Christian faith asserted themselves in theology. At the same time, there were thinkers who opposed this crossing of departmental frontiers and frequently reacted by adopting an attitude of anti-intellectualism. The conflict between the intellectualists and the anti-intellectualists forms one of the most important aspects of philosophical and theological life in the eleventh century.

This contrast is particularly marked in the figures of BERENGARIUS OF TOURS (998–1088) and PETER DAMIAN (1007–1072). Berengarius appears to have put the intellect above authority even in matters of faith. Peter Damian, on the other hand, rejected the use of dialectic in these matters, taking the standpoint that nothing can be known with certainty by the intellect in a natural manner and that knowledge can only be attained with the help of revelation. The problem of the relationship between faith and knowing continued to be one of the centrally important questions of scholastic thought. Neither of the two extreme points of view provided a completely satisfactory answer. The first reconciliatory step was taken by LANFRANC (1005–1089), the abbot of Bec in Normandy who later became Archbishop of Canterbury. He maintained that there was no essential conflict between the divine mysteries and the use of dialectic which could support and confirm these mysteries. Anselm, who succeeded Lanfranc to the see of Canterbury, also followed this line of thought.

Another extremely important aspect of eleventh-century philosophy must also be mentioned at this point. This is the controversy about the ontological value of universal concepts. It has often been claimed that the whole of medieval philosophy arose from this controversy. This is certainly not the case. It is, however, true to say that this controversy strongly influenced the development of the medieval theory of knowledge and the metaphysics of the Middle Ages. The point of departure for this controversy was a passage in Boethius' translation of Porphyry's *Introduction,* in which the question was discussed as to whether the *universalia*—the universal concepts—really existed in or outside things or whether they were nothing more than the products of our mind.

At the end of the eleventh century and the beginning of the twelfth, two men were prominent in this controversy, each maintaining an extreme opinion. The first, WILLIAM OF CHAMPEAUX, upheld the view known as ultra-realism, that is, that the essence of the species is common to all individuals, who are distinguishable from each other only by their accidents, their inessential properties. The second, ROSCELIN OF COMPIÈGNE, attributed reality only to the individual, universality being possessed only by the word which we use to refer to an individual of a certain species. A universal term was therefore a *flatus vocis*, a mere word (nominalism). Most of the early medieval thinkers tended to support the position taken by William of Champeaux. In any attempt to make a true assessment of the viewpoints of both these men, it is important to bear in mind that our knowledge both of William and of Roscelin is mainly derived from the writings of those who opposed them, so that it is difficult to know precisely what they believed. It is nonetheless fairly clear that they were both extremists and therefore doomed to disappear as soon as a greater thinker emerged who was able to present both these conflicting views in a deeper unity. This was in fact done by Peter Abélard.

2. *The Twelfth Century*

The twelfth century was a time of greater political and social stability and this led to the rapid establishment of a flourishing civilization which was also encouraged by the Church. In the early part of the century, those concerned with philosophy were preoccupied with the search for a firm direction which would make enquiry at a more profound level possible. They consequently attempted to find answers to the two questions to which I have alluded in the preceding section. Anselm of Canterbury provided an answer to the first of these questions —that of the relationship between faith and reason (dialectic)— which was to determine philosophical thought for a century and a half and which still continued to be important for a long time after this. Peter Abélard's answer to the second—the question of the *universalia*—was adopted by all the great scholastics and played an important part in all problems connected with the theory of knowledge and ontology in the High Middle Ages.

ANSELM OF CANTERBURY was born at Aosta in 1033. In 1078, he succeeded Lanfranc as abbot of Bec in Normandy and in 1093 succeeded him as Archbishop of Canterbury, where he died in 1109. Although most of his writings date from the eleventh century, his synthetic thought and his great influence on later scholasticism give us every reason for regarding him as a twelfth-century thinker. Anselm fully accepted the use of dialectic in theology. This did not mean for him that reason alone could lead to faith, but rather the contrary—that faith was necessary to a true concept of reality. His view of the relationship between faith and reason was expressed in the concise formula *fides quaerens intellectum*, faith which seeks understanding. Sometimes he expressed this idea more personally as 'I believe in order to understand' (*credo ut intelligam*). In Anselm's view, it was faith which gave the Christian his vision of the world and deeper faith meant a deeper penetration into this vision and thus a deeper understanding of the total reality of God, man and the world. In the centuries that followed, this view dominated the neo-Platonic direction of thought and mysticism. It was also not rejected by the Aristotelian tendency, but given a new shade of meaning.

There is a close connection between this view and Anselm's famous ontological proof of the existence of God. Both were set out in his *Proslogion*. Previously, he had constructed two proofs (in his *Monologion*), in which he had decided on a highest Good and a highest Being from the existence of finite goods and finite beings. In the *Proslogion*, he followed another course. What we mean by God is a being that is greater than any other being that can be thought (*id quo nihil maius cogitari potest*). When we think about God, we have this concept in mind. This concept of God therefore exists in thought, since it is impossible not to think it. But it is clear that something that not only exists in thought but also in reality is greater than something that exists only in thought. If God is really the greatest being that can be thought, he must therefore exist not only in our thought, but also in reality.

A contemporary, Gaunilon, objected to this reasoning in his *Liber pro Insipiente* (*Answer for the Fool*). If something can be thought by the intellect, he argued, it does not follow that it also exists in reality. Otherwise, the concept of an island that is more excellent than all other islands would have to correspond to some reality. In his *Liber apologeticus*, Anselm replied that the concept of God was quite different from any other concept. It was, he maintained, only true of the concept of God, as the concept above which it was impossible to think, that the concept necessarily implied a corresponding reality. We have this concept as a fact, and there would be an inner contradiction if it did not correspond to any reality. This concept of God points to God as the infinite being and it is clear that an infinite being includes real existence. The reality of the existence of God therefore is a consequence of the *factual* presence of our concept of God.

Anselm's *Dialogus de veritate* is another very important work. Regarding it as characteristic of truth that it corresponds to a norm, he referred to the truth of judgement, of thought, of being, of will and of action. In all these forms of truth, it was, in his view, always possible to distinguish a threefold manner of being true—firstly God, who was the creator of truth, secondly the things of the world which were truth created according to the divine norm and thirdly knowledge, which was truth in seeing the manner in which things are related to God. In his dialogue, *De libero arbitrio*, Anselm worked out, in the same spirit, the problem of the freedom of will which was, in his view, essentially a following of the divine norm.

Anselm's theological writings had a very great influence on

the later development of theology. He regarded himself—correctly—as continuing along the lines of Augustine's thought and he even matched Augustine in the personal warmth of his style. Augustine's influence on medieval thought was considerably strengthened by Anselm. After Anselm, the importance of dialectic for theology was universally recognized. In a few works, he made a contribution to the solution of the problem of the *universalia*. In general, however, his thought was in the tradition of ultrarealism. His ontological proof of the existence of God is also closely related to this type of thought. It was Abélard's achievement to show the way in the problem of the *universalia*.

PETER ABÉLARD was born in 1079 at Le Pallet near Nantes. His fierce temperament often caused him to collide headlong with other thinkers and the authorities in the Church. His unhappy love affair with Héloïse was also the cause of great difficulties. After directing a school in Paris for some time, during which dialectic was central to teaching, he began, in 1113, to teach theology. His teaching on the Trinity was condemned in 1121 at the Council of Soissons. In 1136, he resumed teaching at Paris and attracted very many students until he was condemned again in 1141 by the Council of Sens. He then withdrew from the world at Cluny, where he was offered shelter by his friend, Petrus Venerabilis, the abbot. He died in 1142 at the monastery of St Michael at Châlon-sur-Saône. Although he was clearly a convinced Christian, his theological writings often reveal unbalanced judgements. This is due not only to the severe opposition that he encountered, but also to his incomplete grasp of the theological knowledge of his time. His most important achievements were, on the one hand, in the sphere of renewal of method and, on the other, in thinking out burning dialectical problems. His most important works were concerned with fundamental problems of logic and ethics. His autobiography, *The Story of My Adversities* (*Historia calamitatum*), and his correspondence with Héloïse are very important for our knowledge of his life.

Abélard provided a solution to the problem of the *universalia* which set the trend for scholasticism in the High Middle Ages. He was in the favourable position of having been taught both by Roscelin of Compiègne and by William of Champeaux, whose life he had made so burdensome that he had driven him to withdraw into the abbey of St Victor. Abélard opposed Roscelin's doctrine of the Trinity, but could not himself find the right way in this matter. In the sphere of dialectic, however, he broke entirely new ground. Although his knowledge of Aristotle was not great, his solution here was nonetheless Aristotelian. Only the individual is real in the fullest sense of the word. The concepts and names of genera and species are, however, not arbitrary products of the human mind. These concepts refer to qualities that are really present in individual beings. But these qualities have no reality *outside* the individuals, as the ultrarealists believed. In the individuals, however, they are real, with the result that the *universalia* are not, as the nominalists believed, a *flatus vocis*, but real aspects of individual beings. With this form of abstraction, Abélard anticipated the doctrine of abstraction of later Aristotelianism. He stressed that we can conceive the various qualities separately in our thought, but not as *separated* from the individuals to whom they belong: *separatim namque haec res ab alia, non separat intelligitur.*

Whereas thought for Anselm lay within faith, for Abélard it often had a certain degree of independence outside faith. Here, too, he anticipated the Aristotelian scholasticism of the High Middle Ages. Ideas that point to an intellectual preparation for the act of faith can be found in his writings. On the basis of the value that he placed on rational thought as such, Abélard applied the dialectical method without reserve to theology. His *Sic et Non* caused a considerable stir, because in this work he juxtaposed a great number of statements from Scripture and the Church Fathers which were, either apparently or really, contradictory. What is more, he only provided the rules for solving these contradictions, leaving the solutions themselves to his readers. It was therefore obviously not his intention consciously to undermine the authority of the Church, but to attempt to stimulate methodical and dialectical thought.

In the sphere of ethics, Abélard's work was certainly successful in breaking new ground because he was the first to attempt to construct a system of ethics that did not rely on the authority of Scripture. Here, too, he cannot be accused of doubting Christian morality, but it is clear that he believed firmly that Christian morality was an extension of a purely natural morality. The aim of all human activity is the love of God, to which man must aspire. No single action is in itself good or bad but takes its moral value from the inward disposition of man. The ultimate norm of all moral activity is therefore the human conscience. This is also the only norm.

In all these three points, Abélard's influence on later scholastic thought was decisive. His solution to the problem of the *universalia* was generally accepted as 'moderate realism', the dialectical method was universally recognized as the proper preparation for theology and the significance of purely natural ethics was seen in an increasingly clearer light. Abélard's method greatly encouraged the growth of the so-called *Sententiae* literature, in which important theological questions were discussed in the light of biblical or patristic statements. One set of these books of *Sententiae*, the *Senteniarum libri IV* by PETER LOMBARD, had an extraordinary influence throughout the whole of the Middle Ages. The author was moderate and careful but not very original. He was a disciple of Abélard and Hugh of St Victor.

Abélard's teacher, William of Champeaux, withdrew from the conflict with his pupil to the monastery of St Victor in Paris, where he soon resumed teaching. William was certainly not the narrow-minded man that Abélard made him out to be. We may be sure of this because his school of St Victor rapidly achieved fame. The German Hugh was its most famous product.

HUGH OF ST VICTOR (1096–1141) was a many-sided figure, in whom speculative theology and mysticism formed a unity. In addition, he also practised secular science with deep conviction. He valued secular knowledge very highly and, like Anselm, believed that it was ultimately directed towards the knowledge of God. Hugh put forward three proofs of the existence of God. Firstly, God is the creator of the human soul, since this cannot be explained either as eternal or as coming from matter. Secondly, the changing nature of the world requires an unchanging Creator. Finally, everything in the world is directed towards an end, and this final end can only be God. All knowing is brought about by divine illumination. With this illumination theory, Hugh was entirely in the tradition of Anselm and consequently in the Augustinian tradition. Indeed, Hugh's whole psychology, which occupies a very important place in connection with his mysticism, was in the tradition of Augustine. For Hugh, the soul was the human person and the body was only added. The link between the two was of a fortuitous kind.

BERNARD OF CLAIRVAUX (1091–1153) was a friend of the school of St Victor, but he opposed the dialectical method. Although he was involved in all the great religious and political events of his time, Bernard nonetheless managed to lead a life of intense mystical contemplation. His great passion in defending the purity of faith sometimes led him to polemize extremely fiercely and unjustly. His sharp attacks on Abélard are not always admirable. He believed that science was good for the priest in pastoral work, but useless for the monk. Yet he was himself very erudite and sagacious. Many important reflections about questions concerned with the theory of knowledge and anthropology can be found in his works of mystical theology. Unlike Anselm, he laid particular stress on the fact that faith provides full certainty, but remains in itself obscure. He also made an important investigation into human freedom which, in his view, was of necessity always accompanied by insight, but not completely determined by this insight. What is, however, very remarkable is that the anti-humanist and ascetic Bernard had a far more positive attitude towards the relationship between the body and the soul than his friend Hugh of St Victor. For Bernard, the soul and the body were joined in a natural unity (*unio nativa*) which was not external, but essential. This even led him to maintain that perfect happiness in eternal life and the perfect vision of God were possible only after the soul and the body had been re-united. In this, Bernard was one of the first to forsake the Platonic and Augustinian psychology in one extremely important point in favour of a line of reasoning that fitted more closely into the framework of Christian Aristotelianism which was to develop fully in the following century.

The school of Chartres occupied a totally different position in the twelfth century. In the first half of this century, the school was the focal point of humanist thought, a place where the ancient writers were passionately admired and deeply studied and where mathematics, the natural sciences and medicine were also given prominence. The philosophical tendency of this school was strongly Platonic. Unlike the humanism of the school of St Victor, that of Chartres showed a certain tendency towards pantheism. What is more, it is difficult to say anything with certainty about the teaching of the school of Chartres. The many-sided Englishman, JOHN OF SALISBURY (d. 1180), who died as Bishop of Chartres, was a typical example of this twelfth-century humanism.

The precursor of the movement was the Englishman ADELARD OF BATH, who was educated at Tours and Laon and, while travelling in southern Italy, Sicily, Syria and Palestine, became directly acquainted with Greek and Arabic science. The Platonic elements in the school of Chartres may perhaps have come from Adelard, who may have acquired this knowledge in Greek southern Italy. Interest in the atom theory and in empirical natural science, both of which were to be found in the school of Chartres as well as in the school of St Victor, may possibly have originated with Adelard. He began his *De eodem et diverso*, which he wrote between 1105 and 1116 with the affirmation that the science of the ancients was far superior to that of his own time. For him, the philosopher *par excellence* was Plato, but he also seems to have been acquainted with Aristotle. In the problem of the *universalia*, he tried to reconcile Plato and Aristotle. He may possibly have given Abélard some suggestions for his own solution to the problem here. Adelard also referred to the need for a purely scientific method where questions of natural experience were concerned. Apart from Arabic works dealing with mathematics, he also translated Euclid's *Elements*.

This brings us directly to the subject of the increase in knowledge of first sources throughout the twelfth century. In this respect too, the twelfth century was extremely important and in it the foundations were laid for the later structure of scholasticism that was to arise in the High Middle Ages. Thanks to livelier contact with the Greek civilization of southern Italy and Sicily and later on with that of the Byzantine Empire as well, many new translations were made. Contact with the Arabic culture in Spain also led to many other translations— the Archbishop of Toledo even established a special school for translations from Arabic. Thus, not only were writings by Arabic authors translated at this time, but also writings by Greeks that had been translated into Arabic. This resulted in very many Greek texts becoming known in western Europe through Arabic.

In this way, then, translations were made of Plato's *Meno* and *Phaedo*, of the hitherto unknown part of Aristotle's *Organon* (the *logica nova*), of his *Physics*, of *De Anima* and fragments of his *Metaphysics* and his *Nicomachaen Ethics*. Medieval knowledge of the Greek Fathers of the Church was also improved in the same way. The *Liber de causis* also became known at this time. In the sphere of Arabic philosophy, works by Alfarabi, Algazel, Alkindi, Avicenna and Avicebron (a Jew who wrote in Arabic) were translated. These writers juxtaposed Aristotelian and neo-Platonic elements in a frequently original treatment.

Translations also gave a great stimulus to the practice of other sciences—especially jurisprudence, which began to flourish at Bologna, and medicine, which was practised successfully for a long period at Salerno and Montpellier. The school of Orléans became famous for the study of classical literature. Paris became more and more a centre of science and numerous schools arose there. These schools combined at the end of the twelfth century to form the University of Paris. The University of Bologna is possibly somewhat older, but it lacked the manysided activity of the University of Paris. Oxford and Naples soon followed at the beginning of the thirteenth century. It was in the university faculties of the liberal arts and theology that thirteenth-century scholasticism achieved its greatest triumphs.

3. *The Heyday of Neo-Platonism*

Aristotle's influence on philosophy did not extend very far in the early Middle Ages. Until the twelfth century, knowledge of Aristotle was confined to a part of Boethius' translation of and commentary on the *Organon* (the *logica vetus*) and to his translation of and commentary on Porphyry's *Introduction to Aristotle's Categories*. As I have said in the preceding section, a good deal of the rest of Aristotle's work and a number of Arabic and Jewish interpretations of Aristotle, among which the work of Avicenna was paramount, became known in the second half of the twelfth century. Later, in the first half of the thirteenth century, Aristotle's remaining texts were translated and Averroes' commentaries on Aristotle became known. AVERROES (1126–1198) was a Spanish-Arabic philosopher whose thesis that the human intellect was supra-individual became a controversial question in the thirteenth century. At about the same time, the works of MOSES MAIMONIDES (1135–1204) also became known. He was a Jewish philosopher who wrote in Arabic and who attempted to reconcile Aristotelian philosophy with Scripture.

All thirteenth-century philosophers were influenced by Aristotle, but they can be characterized by the way in which they used Aristotelian thought. It is possible to distinguish two main tendencies in broad outline. The first used Aristotelian philosophy as a technical instrument for thought, but retained a number of traditional philosophical attitudes of neo-Platonic and Augustinian origin as against certain contradictory statements of Aristotle. The second tendency was an attempt to incorporate the whole of Aristotelian philosophy into a synthetic pattern of thought, but even here a fair number of traditional elements continued to play an important part.

The general situation in theology especially was that the Augustinian view predominated even among the majority of thinkers who inclined towards Aristotelianism. Alongside this tendency, however, schools of philosophy had grown up during the twelfth century in the faculties of liberal arts, schools which no longer confined themselves exclusively to logic, but gradually enlarged their scope to include psychology, ethics, physics and metaphysics. Such teaching was distinct from the teaching of theology and it was in these schools of philosophy that Aristotelianism made itself most powerfully felt. A 'philosophical view of the world' came about alongside the theological view of the world. Since almost all thinkers of this period first spent several years teaching in the faculty of liberal arts and then transferred to the theological faculty, the influence of Aristotelianism on theology continued to increase. Theologians were conscious of being confronted with the task of incorporating the Aristotelian view of the world into the traditionally Augustinian theological view. It was from this tension that the most important works of the great thirteenth-century thinkers arose. In addition, more and more purely philosophical works were produced as a result of the work of the faculties of liberal arts. The existing distinction between philosophy and theology also led to more and more thought being given to the relationship between philosophy and theology, between understanding and believing. Thus, in the thirteenth century, partly as a consequence of Abélard's preparatory work, philosophy came to exist independently of theology.

But, as I have already indicated, there was, in addition to this Aristotelian influence, also an increased influence from neo-Platonism. The writings of the Pseudo-Dionysius were subjected to even more intense study at this time, and interest in the other great thinkers of Greek patristicism, who were so deeply influenced by neo-Platonism, rapidly increased. Finally, many Aristotelian as well as neo-Platonic theories were taken from the Arabic texts, including the *Liber de causis,* which went back, through Alfarabi, to Proclus. Since all thinkers of this period reveal the influence both of neo-Platonism and of Aristotle, it is extremely difficult to make a consistent distinction between the neo-Platonic Augustinian tendency and the Aristotelian school. I am obliged to characterize each of these movements in very broad terms because of the need to separate them for the purposes of this book.

I would distinguish the following broad characteristics of

the neo-Platonic, Augustinian school of thought: 1. the independence of the soul in respect of the body; 2. the possibility of intellectual knowledge without the aid of the outside world; 3. the need of divine illumination for intellectual knowledge; 4. the trichotomy of the spiritual life into memory, intellect and will; 5. the primacy of the will above the intellect; 6. the separate forms of being for vegetative, sensitive and spiritual life; 7. the composition of all beings, even purely spiritual beings, of form and matter; 8. the impossibility of any eternal creation; and 9. the practical merging of theology and philosophy into one single wisdom.

The Aristotelian tendency, on the other hand, may be characterized thus: 1. the substantial unity of soul and body; 2. the impossibility of intellectual knowledge without the aid of the outside world; 3. the formation of intellectual knowledge by abstraction; 4. the dichotomy of the spiritual life into intellect and will; 5. the primacy of the intellect above the will; 6. the spiritual soul as the only form of being of man; 7. the composition of purely spiritual beings as existence and essence and not as form and matter; 8. the possibility of an eternal creation, and 9. the theoretical and practical recognition of the distinction between theology and philosophy.

It is difficult to insist rigidly on these characteristics because the situation is complicated by various factors. In the first place, there is considerable overlapping of Aristotelian and neo-Platonic, Augustinian characteristics in the case of many thinkers. Secondly, many of them show a development from a neo-Platonic to a more Aristotelian point of view, but also occasionally the opposite movement. Thirdly, we are often prevented by the limited material that has been published from coming to a conclusive verdict. Finally, those thinkers who inclined towards Aristotelianism generally show Augustine's influence much more in their theological works than in their philosophical works. But, judging by the above-mentioned characteristics, it is clear that, in spite of the gradually deepening influence of Aristotle, the predominant influence in the thirteenth century was neo-Platonic and Augustinian. In the first half of the thirteenth century, this latter influence was almost exclusive.

WILLIAM OF AUVERGNE, who was first magister of the theological faculty of the University of Paris and later became Bishop of Paris (1228-49), was the first thinker of real stature in whom the conflict between Aristotelian and traditional philosophical ideas can be detected. Well-read in the traditional literature, in Aristotle and in the Arabic and Jewish writers, William occupies a distinctive place in the history of philosophy. He can be regarded as the forerunner of the great speculative thinkers of the second half of his century both because of his wide erudition and the speculative nature of his theology.

During William's professorship and episcopate at Paris, difficulties arose in connection with the teaching of Aristotle at the University. The theological faculty was alarmed about the unrestrained admiration for Aristotle in the faculty of liberal arts, believing that it threatened orthodoxy. In 1210, a council at Paris forbade lectures to be given on Aristotle's natural philosophical writings or the commentaries on these. This ban was confirmed five years later by the papal legate and it was more precisely defined and extended. The metaphysical writings of Aristotle were banned from lectures as well as the natural philosophical writings, but his logical works were prescribed and his ethics were allowed *ad libitum*. Broadly speaking, this ban seems to have remained in force until about 1240. What is certain is that it was in connection with these difficulties that Pope Gregory IX appointed William of Auvergne Bishop of Paris. This was without doubt an attempt on his part to bring about a reconciliation between the two camps, since the Pope was naturally aware of William's open approach to Aristotle. What is not clear, however, is the part that William continued to play in the conflict. All that is certain is that Gregory IX sent William a letter at the end of 1229, in which he expressed his regret at having appointed him! This, however, was connected with other difficulties, in particular a general strike that had broken out that year among the students and teachers of the University as the result of a quarrel with an inn-keeper. The partial ban on the teaching of Aristotle and the general strike gravely damaged the reputation of the University, and the University of Toulouse, which was founded in 1229, issued at the end of that year a prospectus in which it advertised courses on the writings of Aristotle that were banned in Paris!

The practical outcome of this situation, however, was that the University of Oxford became the centre of Aristotelian studies in the first half of the thirteenth century. The leading light in the study of Aristotle at Oxford at this time seems to have been ROBERT GROSSETESTE (c. 1170–1253). Robert, who was born in Suffolk, became a professor and, later, Chancellor of the University. From 1229 until 1232, he was Archdeacon of Leicester and, from 1232 until his death, he was Bishop of Lincoln. He translated the *Nichomachean Ethics* from the original Greek and commented on the *Physics* and some of Aristotle's works of logic. In addition to this, he also wrote a commentary on the works of the Pseudo-Dionysius. His own works were strongly neo-Platonic in character. The theory of spiritual and material illumination as the essential form of spiritual and material beings was at the centre of his thought. Two striking aspects of Robert's activity were his predilection for mathematical formulae and his practice of experimental science. Here, too, he gave the University of Oxford its direction. Many of Robert's publications were concerned with empiricism, in which he anticipated his pupil Roger Bacon.

During the episcopate of William of Auvergne, the most

important figure at the faculty of theology in Paris was
ALEXANDER OF HALES (c. 1175–1245). Although he was born
in Gloucestershire, he seems to have studied at Paris. Afterwards, he taught first in the faculty of liberal arts and then in
the theological faculty of Paris. In 1231, he became a Franciscan
and at this period he and his disciple, JOHN OF RUPELLA (Jean
de la Rochelle, 1200–45), were the leading representatives
of the policy of energetic study in the Franciscan order.
Although he was well acquainted with the works of Aristotle,
he remained generally speaking faithful to the neo-Platonic,
Augustinian tradition—this is clear from his great work, the
Summa universae theologicae.

In the meantime, the situation at the University of Paris
had changed considerably. Gregory IX had succeeded in
settling the general strike, but he maintained his ban on
Aristotle's natural philosophical works, saying in his letter
that this would remain in force 'until they had been investigated and purified of all suspicion of error'. Gregory appointed
a commission to examine Aristotle's works, but it was not able
to complete its work. It is clear from this that he wanted
gradually to reintroduce Aristotle into the University syllabus.
Although they were repeated later, it is obvious that, from
1240 onwards, the bans were regarded as no longer being in
force.

Foremost among neo-Platonic, Augustinian thinkers in the
second half of the thirteenth century were Roger Bacon and
Saint Bonaventure. Although Bacon was some ten years older
than Bonaventure and the latter probably attended Bacon's
lectures on Aristotle in Paris, there is every reason for dealing
with Bonaventure's philosophy first. Giovanni Fidanza, who
was nicknamed BONAVENTURE, was born near Viterbo in
1221 and studied in Paris, where he became a Franciscan. He
was taught by Alexander of Hales and John of Rupella and
taught himself at the theological faculty from 1248 until 1257,

when he was elected General of his order. At intervals, however, he gave lectures at Paris, his last being in the spring of 1274. He died later in the year at the end of the Council of Lyons.

Bonaventure's academic career was in fact very short—it was broken off when he became General of the Franciscan order. This career was also confined entirely to the sphere of theology. He never taught in the faculty of liberal arts—his earliest teaching was done in the theological faculty and his later work shows that he was just as much a theologian at the end of his life. His philosophical ideas have to be traced within the framework of his theology, and this is all the more difficult because he in principle never accorded an independent role to philosophy. He was an outstanding stylist who can still hold the reader's attention with his clear, warm style and who always goes straight to the heart of the matter.

Although Bonaventure was first and foremost a theologian, he was fully in touch with the philosophical trends of his own time. Even in his earliest works, it is clear that he was familiar with Aristotle and with the Arabic and Jewish interpreters of Aristotle. But, from the very beginning, he preserved a great measure of independence. His attitude was simply that he would not give up any traditional position (in his case, the neo-Platonic Augustinian) unless he was completely convinced of the superiority of the opposite position. And he was never convinced of the superiority of the Aristotelian position in any single point. The nine affirmations which I have given previously as characteristic of the neo-Platonic, Augustinian school of thought are all to be found in his works. There is possibly no other scholastic thinker who took the relationship between life, thought, faith and action more deeply into account, but it is at the same time clear that the relative independence of thought to a great extent escaped him. Bonaventure's doctrine was a consistent elaboration of Anselm's *credo ut intelligam*. Although he made constant use of Aristotelian terms and concepts, he never really fully considered the inner relationship between these concepts. The unity of Bonaventure's theology is not founded on a unity of consistently thought out philosophy. He was only interested in what he could use for his theological synthesis. This, however, does not mean that he slavishly followed tradition. His view was extremely personal and he was as critical of the traditional theologians, such as Peter Lombard, as he was of Aristotelian thinkers.

Bonaventure claimed that the existence of God could be proved in many ways. If the soul returned upon itself, it became aware of God's presence in itself. Furthermore, how could our inconstant and changeable mind reach unchangeable judgements if it were not for God's illumination? God's presence was therefore, Bonaventure argued, contained in every form of knowledge. He went on, in the spirit of Anselm, to argue further that we certainly knew God in one way or another. But how should this knowledge of God exist if there were no God? Finally, Bonaventure insisted, God's existence was clear from the whole of nature, which presupposed God as its final explanation.

Having established the existence of God, Bonaventure maintained, it is then possible to discuss the essence of things. If God exists, he reasoned, he is the Creator and all else is created. It is impossible for this creation to be eternal (as Aristotle and Averroes asserted), since an eternal creation would be an inner contradiction. But, if God's creation is from nothing, then it must be, in one way or another, a reflection of its Creator. Created by God, it must, as a faithful reflection of the Creator, return to the Creator. This return is not a removal of the infinite distance between the Creator and his creation, but the attainment of creation's real aim— the glorification of the Creator. Nature glorifies God simply by the fact of its existence. Man must glorify God in freedom, by striving to be a more pure reflection of God.

All created beings, even purely spiritual beings, are composed of matter and form. Form and matter, act and potency are identical pairs of concepts. Only God is pure act or pure form and only purely spiritual beings (the angels) are composed of matter and one single form. All other beings have several forms, even man, whose dignity is determined by the highest form, reason. Reason enables man to share in God's being. Like Robert Grosseteste, Bonaventure also liked to speak about light as a form of being.

As far as the world of the senses was concerned, Bonaventure fully accepted Aristotelianism. In the perceptible world, the senses had an essential part to play—the intellect obtained its knowledge by abstraction. But this was not the case with knowledge of the soul and of God. Here, sensory knowledge and abstraction were, in Bonaventure's view, quite insufficient. The soul knows itself only by returning upon itself and, turning thus inwards, it also finds God. This is not a question of abstraction, but of divine illumination. The soul therefore has a manner of knowing that is independent of the body. For Bonaventure, then, the soul was an independent entity that was united with the body. The principle of individuality was not to be found either in the soul (form) or in the body (matter), but in the special manner in which any given soul and body were joined in any given being.

Bonaventure handed the tradition of Franciscan thought which began with Alexander of Hales on to the later thinkers of his order until it reached a new peak in Duns Scotus. Another important figure was the Englishman JOHN PECKHAM, who was born about 1230, studied in Paris under Bonaventure and later became a professor himself at Paris and Oxford. In 1279, he became Archbishop of Canterbury and did everything that he could to uphold the traditional Augustinianism in the face of the rising tide of Thomism until his death in 1292. His works, which have so far only been published in part, reveal a powerful thinker who was, generally speaking, faithful to the Bonaventuran tradition and who defended Bonaventure's views against Thomism. The Italian MATTHEW OF AQUASPARTA was even clearer and more profound than Peckham. He was born about 1240, became General of the Franciscan order in 1287 and in 1288, Cardinal Archbishop of Porto. He died in 1302. His written works have contributed a great deal to the clarification and deeper understanding of Bonaventure whom, broadly speaking, he followed faithfully. In many of his theories, he anticipated Duns Scotus. Unlike Bonaventure, he held that the soul and the body formed a substantial unity, a view which he took over from Thomas Aquinas.

In the thirteenth century, neo-Platonic Augustinianism was defended by the Franciscans especially, but there were also many Dominicans and members of the secular clergy who supported it. The most important of these in the second half of the thirteenth century was HENRY OF GHENT (c. 1217–1293), who taught in the theological faculty and played a leading part in the life of the University. Henry was a very independent thinker who, like Thomas Aquinas, acknowledged that philosophy had its own important part to play. The distinction that he made between philosophy and theology was that philosophy was the science of the natural and theology was the science of the supernatural. Philosophical knowledge of God was, in his view, only possible through the medium of creation. Like Thomas, he rejected the theory of several forms being contained in the same being and the composition of pure spirits of form and matter. In this, he departed radically from the Franciscan tradition, but he nonetheless remained faithful to most of the philosophical attitudes that went back directly to Augustine. For him, the soul was a separate substance from the body. Intellectual knowledge was only set in motion by sensory experience, but owed its content to innate ideas or to divine illumination. Henry was very conscious of the difficulty of explaining the concrete aspect of knowledge on the basis of this view and his efforts to solve this problem suggested certain ideas to him which were later taken over and more fully worked out by Duns Scotus on the one hand and William of Ockham on the other. He laid even more stress than Bonaventure on the will as the most important of the human faculties, and this emphasis on the will distinguishes him sharply from Thomas Aquinas, who stressed the intellect.

ROGER BACON was born at Ilchester about 1212. He was a disciple of Robert Grosseteste and, in 1245 or thereabouts, interpreted Aristotle's *Physics* and *Metaphysics* at the faculty of liberal arts, where Bonaventure may have followed his lectures. Somewhere about the year 1250, he entered the Franciscan order and taught at Oxford until 1257, when he gave up teaching because of difficulties with his superiors. He continued, however, to pursue experimental, philosophical and theological studies privately. At the request of Pope Clement IV, he wrote his *Opus maius*. The individual subjects which Roger deals with in each of the seven parts of this work reveal his wide-ranging interests. Part 1 deals with the causes of our errors, Part 2 with the relationships between philosophy and the sciences and theology, Part 3 with the need for a knowledge of languages, Part 4 with mathematics, astronomy and astrology, Part 5 with optics, Part 6 with experimental science and Part 7 with moral philosophy as a way to God. When Bishop Tempier of Paris condemned astrology together with a number of Averroist ideas, Bacon wrote his *Speculum astronomiae*. In this book he spared nobody—even Albert the Great, whose thinking was closely related to his own, came in for some particularly hard knocks. He expressed the view that everything was in a state of decline and that the end of the world was approaching. The work was condemned and Roger was deprived of his freedom of movement, which was only given back to him shortly before his death, in 1292. Large parts of his *Opus minus* and *Opus tertius* were already contained in his *Opus maius*. Besides these, however, the *Opus minus* contains a treatment of speculative alchemy and a study of the causes of the decline of theology and the *Opus tertius* deals with new experimental problems and provides many autobiographical details. Apart from these three comprehensive works, we have a number of lesser works by Bacon which have not yet been published in full.

Roger Bacon was a very mysterious figure. A turbulent character who came into conflict with everyone, he was always looking for new paths to follow in experimental science while he was at the same time an excellent linguist who was constantly criticizing his contemporaries for their lack of knowledge of languages. But for all this, and despite his reverence for Aristotle, he was rather conservative in his speculative thought. He seems not to have understood at all the real struggle to develop an independent philosophy with the help of Aristotelian principles, as conducted by Albert the Great and Thomas Aquinas. On the other hand, however, he made very definite achievements in the sphere of positive science and never overlooked the connection between this branch of learning and the whole. It is becoming increasingly clear that Roger Bacon and Albert the Great were the most important representatives of a great movement which began in the twelfth century and which initiated the development of modern philological and experimental science. It is also certain that this movement was stronger in Oxford (with Robert Grosseteste, for example) than in Paris.

It is possible that Bacon influenced the work of the Spaniard RAYMOND LULL (*c.* 1235–1315), the poet, writer of romances, philosopher, theologian, apologist of the Church and opponent of Islam and Averroism, logician and philologist who himself wrote, not only in Latin, but also in Catalan and Arabic. As in the case of Bacon and Bonaventure, all learning was for him at the service of the one wisdom, the Christian faith. He used his study of logic, which is to be found in many of his works, but especially in his *Ars Magna,* to combat the Mohammedans and the Averroists. These studies in logic were of great importance in the later history of the science—Leibniz in particular was deeply influenced by them.

JOHN DUNS SCOTUS was born in Scotland in 1266. He entered the order of Friars Minor and studied at Cambridge, Oxford and Paris. Afterwards, he taught alternately at Oxford and Paris. He died in 1308. Very many unauthenticated works have been attributed to Scotus. His critical depth and his extremely concise style make his work difficult to understand. In addition, part of his genuine literary output has not yet been published, and what is available is in very bad condition. In the past, Scotus was not held in very high esteem, but now that his authentic works have been separated from those that are not genuine, it is clear that he was a very constructive thinker of great stature. He used his repeated criticisms of most of his contemporaries, especially the Averroists, but also Roger Bacon, Thomas Aquinas, Giles of Rome (Aegidius Romanus), Henry of Ghent and others, to build up his own system of thought. He clearly aimed to continue in the tradition of Franciscan thought, but at the same time to vindicate this tradition rationally and fully in the eyes of the great thinkers of his own day. This ultimately led him to become much more of an Aristotelian than Bonaventure and to take up what was to some extent a middle position between Thomas and Bonaventure. His attitude testifies to a great power of thought, although it cannot be said that he succeeded in combining the most profound ideas of both of these thinkers in a new synthesis and in going farther than they had gone.

According to Scotus, the intellect is directed towards being as such. But, in this life, the intellect is tied to sensory perception, because the soul is tied to the body. Whereas all knowledge in this life has to begin with sensory perception, the soul that is freed from the body does not have to follow this devious course. But, as far as this life is concerned, we are bound to accept the abstraction of knowledge, and Scotus therefore rejected the Augustinian theory of illumination. But he accepted that the doctrine of abstraction required amplification, since, even if it were true that there are no separate essences corresponding to the abstracted aspects of beings, the abstraction is not arbitrary and there is something to provide a basis in beings for this abstraction. The abstracted aspects are thus neither really different nor really identical. Scotus referred to this as a *distinctio formalis*.

But, if the intellect is directed towards being as such, what then is this being? For Scotus, being is the most universal and therefore the poorest concept, without positive content and meaning only 'not nothing'—*esse se extendit ad quodcumque quod non est nihil*. According to Scotus, this concept of being is identical in all its applications—being is univocal. This does not, however, mean, Scotus argued, that every being does not have its own mode of being—on the contrary, *omne esse habet aliquod esse proprium*. For this reason, no single being can be fully grasped in universal concepts. All being is individual—each being is this specific being. Being is therefore not individualized either by form or by matter, but by being this as such (*haecceitas*).

It follows from the pluriformity, fortuitousness and composite nature of the things that surround us, Scotus argued, that God exists. What is pluriform, fortuitous and composite, however, presupposes what is one, necessary and non-composite. The outstanding characteristic of everything that is fortuitous is finiteness. Infinity is therefore the outstanding characteristic of God. The infinite being is the being which necessarily exists. The concept of an infinite being, Scotus reasoned with Anselm, is a proof for the existence of that infinite being. This infinite being can only be a spiritual being, since matter implies divisibility and therefore finiteness. God is therefore pre-eminently intellect and will, which are inseparable in God, but which have to be separated in the light of our knowledge—*Deus rationabilissime vult,* God wills in the most reasonable way.

God is the cause and the end of all beings, which are created according to the model of his essence and, in so far as they are rational, must direct themselves towards this model of God's essence. In a certain sense, therefore, the will is man's highest faculty, because it is with his will that man can freely turn towards God. The will motivates the intellect, although intellectual judgement about truth and falsehood can only proceed from the intellect.

Scotus rejected Anselm's *credo ut intelligam*—faith and understanding were for him two totally different things. He attributed a great deal to faith that could, according to other scholastics, also be understood. He was also influenced by the mathematical and experimental studies that were going on at Oxford. The highest demonstrability was for him that of mathematics—no other science could be proved to such perfection. Metaphysical argument was less stringent, although it had to do with more important matters. The same applied, Scotus held, to ethics. For him, only proper reverence for God resulted from the essence of the relationship between the Creator and the creature; the other ethical norms he regarded as positive directions which were dependent on God's will.

4. *The Heyday of Aristotelianism*

Although it is very difficult to draw a clear dividing line here, it is nonetheless customary to distinguish an Augustinian and an Aristotelian tendency in thirteenth-century thought. This terminology, however, can easily lead to confusion. As

I have already said, the background to the thought of all the great thirteenth-century philosophers and theologians was Augustinian. It is, however, possible to say that, in the practical working out of this Augustinian thought, there were two main tendencies, the one being predominantly neo-Platonic, the other Aristotelian. That is why I regard it as incorrect to use the terms Augustinianism and Aristotelianism and prefer to speak of neo-Platonic Augustinianism and Aristotelian Augustinianism. In this way, it is possible to do justice to the influence of St Augustine on the whole of medieval thought, an influence which is greater than that of any other thinker. But, although this terminology is preferable, it should not be forgotten that very many of Aristotle's ideas were assimilated into the thought of the neo-Platonic Augustinian school and that the Aristotelian Augustinian tendency was also strongly influenced by neo-Platonic thought. What all this really comes to is that the philosophy of the greatest medieval thinkers provides an original synthesis which cannot be fitted into the framework of ancient or patristic thought.

The first thinker who was influenced more by Aristotelian than by neo-Platonic ideas was ALBERT THE GREAT. Albert, who was born in 1206 at Lauingen in Swabia, studied the liberal arts at the University of Padua and entered the Dominican order in 1223. He continued his studies in Cologne, where he began to teach theology as early as 1228. After teaching in various other German cities, he moved to Paris and gave lectures there between 1240 and 1248. He returned to Cologne in 1248 to establish a Studium Generale for the Dominicans. From 1254 to 1257 he was the Provincial of the German province of his order. He resumed lecturing at Cologne in 1257, but became Bishop of Ratisbon in 1260. Two years later he became a papal legate, but, despite the many missions that he had to undertake, he still managed to find time for study. He died at Cologne in 1280. The years that Albert spent in Paris must have been of the greatest importance to him. William of Auvergne was at that time the Bishop of Paris; Alexander of Hales and John of Rupella were lecturing there and Roger Bacon was teaching for the first time since the ban on Aristotle's *Physics* and *Metaphysics*.

Albert occupies a very remarkable place in the history of philosophy. With Roger Bacon, he was the leading representative of his age in the sphere of experimental science. He did more than any other thinker to make the West familiar with the philosophy of Aristotle. At the same time, however, he remained faithful to many aspects of neo-Platonic thought and even strengthened the neo-Platonic influence by his exposition of the Pseudo-Dionysius. It is quite clear from his work not only that he regarded experiment as necessary in all the natural sciences, but also that he himself systematically practised experiment and observation. This is particularly evident in his botanical, biological, geographical and astronomical writings which are often extremely accurate, display a very realistic attitude and were clearly based on his own observations. Thus, he frequently criticized Aristotle whenever the data provided by the Greek thinker did not tally with his own observations. Very many of the views that were prevalent at the time, such as the current view that the southern hemisphere was uninhabitable, were challenged by Albert whose arguments were always extremely objective.

Albert made a much clearer distinction than any of the thinkers of the neo-Platonic Augustinian school between philosophy and theology. Philosophy, he maintained, worked with the light of the natural intellect that is given to all men, whereas theology relied on the data of faith. Because of this distinction, philosophy was for Albert an independent science which could be of great service to theology, but which derived its own value from itself.

Albert used the Aristotelian idea of the Prime Mover as a

proof of the existence of God. If this Prime Mover really was the first principle of everything, Albert argued, then he must be absolutely necessary Being that is pure Act without any potency. This pure act is pure Intellect knowing itself. This Aristotelian idea was supplemented in Albert's reasoning by the idea of the Pseudo-Dionysius that all our names for God are insufficient because God infinitely transcends all our names and concepts.

In his explanation of the creation, Albert followed the neo-Platonic theory of emanation of the *Liber de causis*, attempting at the same time to preserve the Christian idea of creation from nothing. He agreed with the Aristotelians that intellect alone cannot demonstrate that creation is not eternal, although he did not accept this view during his early period. He was also in agreement with them in rejecting the idea that pure spirits and the human soul were composed of form and matter and in accepting the theory of abstraction. In his treatise against Averroes, he argued that the individuality of each human being presupposes the individuality of the human soul and thus also the individuality of the human intellect, with the conclusion that Averroes' assertion of the superindividual unity of the human intellect was, in his opinion, untenable. This individuality of the human soul which, in view of its intellectual performance, transcends matter cannot therefore be subject to material decomposition and the individual immortality of the human soul is thus guaranteed.

Albert never developed his philosophical ideas into a carefully thought out schematic whole, but his open-minded attitude towards philosophy prepared the way for Thomas Aquinas' synthesis and his researches pointed the way to further experimental research on the part of later thinkers.

The Aristotelian trend in Albert's thought was continued by THOMAS AQUINAS, in whom medieval philosophy reached its highest point. Thomas was born in 1225 at Rocca Secca near Aquino in Campania. As early as the autumn of 1239, he was enrolled as a student in the faculty of liberal arts of the University of Naples, where, in the spring of 1244, he became a Dominican and studied from 1245 to 1248 under Albert the Great in Paris. He followed Albert to Cologne, where he remained until returning to Paris in 1252. He taught at the theological faculty there until 1259, first as a baccalaureus, but, from 1256 onwards, as a magister.

Even in this early period, it is clear that Thomas had already chosen the philosophical path that he was to follow. He was able to distinguish more clearly than any of his contemporaries between the Aristotelian and the neo-Platonic elements in the new literature. After stripping them of later additions, he accepted without hesitation certain basic Aristotelian ideas. He completely rejected the theory of illumination, maintaining that our knowledge was acquired by abstraction from sensory perceptions. Aristotle's theory of act and potency was extended metaphysically by Thomas and, like the more special theory of hylomorphism, stripped of later Stoic and neo-Platonic elements. The main trends in Thomas's thinking were thus firmly established even at this time. It is, however, clear from the beginning that Thomas's synthesis was not simply a reproduction of Aristotle's philosophy. He succeeded in fusing neo-Platonic Augustinian and Aristotelian elements into a highly original synthesis. There is no trace of philosophic eclecticism in Thomas's thought, as was the case even with great thinkers such as Bonaventure and Albert. Every philosophical idea was thought out by Thomas in its unity with other fundamental ideas. The Aristotelian Augustinian characteristic certainly applies to Thomas's thought, which upheld Platonic Augustinian participation as the most fundamental philosophic idea. But, as with all very original thinking, it is also true of Thomas's thought that its characteristics were not entirely derived from what had gone before in philosophy and that his synthesis was neither Aristotelian nor Augustinian, but simply Thomist.

From 1259 until 1264, Thomas taught at the papal court at Anagni and Orvieto. From 1265 to 1267, he taught at Rome and then, from the end of 1267 until the beginning of 1269, he taught again at the papal court at Viterbo. During this period, he became acquainted with the Flemish Dominican, William of Moerbeke, whom he asked for better translations of Aristotle. From the beginning of 1269 until Easter 1272, Thomas was again teaching at Paris. He returned to Naples in 1272, in order to set up a Studium Generale for the Dominicans. He was taken ill on the way to the Council of Lyons and died on 7 March 1274 in the abbey of Fossanova.

There is a gradual development in Thomas's writings in the increasingly deeper effect on his thought of the Aristotelian viewpoint that he accepted from the very beginning. Thus there is a noticeable difference between what he wrote before 1260 and what he wrote after this date, when he was continuously engaged on his commentaries on Aristotle. It is, however, not possible to deal with this historical factor in this brief consideration of Thomas's thought and I shall confine myself to an outline of his synthesis, with special attention to the *Summa Theologica*.

The Platonic, Augustinian idea of participation is basic to Thomas's thought. All created being is a participation in God's being. The basis of this participation is, however, not to be found in a neo-Platonic emanation, in which the universe proceeds gradually from the deity, but in the fact of creation. Thomas insisted on an act of creation by which God produces the created world from nothing. In this, he emphasized two things from the very outset. In the first place, God creates from nothing. There is therefore no primordial duality between God (good) and matter (evil), as was maintained by all forms of Gnosticism. Since everything proceeds by creation from

God, everything also shares in God's goodness and the material world also has its own form of goodness. In the second place, creation is not an act which took place at a particular moment of time, after which the created world was left to its fate. Creation is the continuous production and preservation of the accidental by the Necessary. Creation, which does not explain itself, can only find an ultimate explanation in God who necessarily exists and therefore has no need of an explanation from outside. God therefore creates from eternity both the universe and time. Thus the idea of creation is not invalidated by an eternal world. Although Scripture teaches that the world had a beginning, philosophy is not capable of proving this, just as it is not capable of proving that the world had no beginning.

If the universe is created by God and is therefore not itself God, what, then, is the mode of being of this universe? If God is as the Creator and the universe is as the created, what is the difference between them? Creation is a participation in God's being. This participation, however, is not quantitative, rather as if every created being represented a little part of the deity. All that this participation means is that there is a certain analogy between the Creator and creation. The Creator can only communicate his own goodness to creation. Analogy means similarity and difference in the same and it is not concerned with accidentals, but only with the most essential, in other words, with the being of God and the world. It also implies that there is an infinite distance between the Creator's being and that of creation, but that, despite this infinite distance, creation in some way shares in God's being.

Of what does this sharing in God's being consist? In the first place, it is to be found in the creature's being as such. As a being, the creature necessarily shares in the *transcendentalia* of all being—unity, truth and goodness. In so far as it is, every creature is one, true and good. Even more important, however, is the question, what is the difference between God's uncreated being and the world's created being? This difference is to be found in the fact that God *is* his being and that the creature *has* its being. In other words, in God, existence and being are completely identical, whereas there is a metaphysical distinction between existence and essence in the creature. This metaphysical distinction does not mean that there is a physical divisibility, but that the creature's essence does not include its existence. The creature is thus metaphysically composed of existence and essence.

Thomas, however, went farther than this and placed the (neo-) Platonic idea of participation within a framework of Aristotelian concepts, seeing the composition of existence and essence as a first form of the composition of act and potency. The Creator is pure Act and the pure spiritual creatures (the angels) are composed of existence and essence. They have no further composition—there is no distinction between matter and form in their being. In their case, therefore, there can also be no question of individuation within one species—each angel is his own species. It is only in the material beings— lifeless things, plants, animals and human beings—that there is, in addition to a composition of existence and essence which characterizes the state of being a creature has as such, a composition of form (act) and matter (potency), which is therefore the characteristic of all material beings. This composition not only makes material change possible, but also individuation. The quantitative divisibility of matter makes it possible for the same species (form) to be realized in different individuals. This does not mean that these individuals all possess only one form—as Averroes attributed only one intellect to all men— but that these individuals are different realizations of one form which is ideally the same. In reality, however, every being is individual, both in its form and in its matter, but on the basis of matter.

Man's being can therefore be defined more precisely. Man is above all a unity, an independent unit, consisting of form (the soul) and matter (the body). The soul is not a separate independent unit, as was taught by the Platonists, but what animates and inspires the body. Among the activities of which man is capable, there are, however, some, like those of thought and the will, which transcend his purely physical nature. The soul cannot therefore perish with man's body at death, but must continue to exist. But this does not mean that every action performed in this life—even an act of thought or of the will—is not an action of the whole person, of the 'I' that is a unity of body and soul. Thus, my intellect does not think, nor does my eye see, but, on the contrary, I think and I see. This human unity, which carries out every human act, therefore presupposes that the human body is animated by only one (spiritual) form, which at the same time informs the vegetative life of the senses. It is unnecessary to assume any further forms of being in man.

If, then, the soul forms a unity with the body, it is also not independent of the body in its knowledge. There is therefore no knowledge which does not, in one way or another, have its point of departure in the senses. All intellectual knowledge is attained by abstraction from sensory knowledge. A first abstraction disregards the individual characteristics of things and thus makes natural science possible. A second abstraction regards only the quantity of things and thus leads to the science of mathematics. A third abstraction is concerned only with the being of things and thus forms the point of departure for metaphysics. Since it also abstracts from the specifically material, this science makes it possible for us to think about God.

Knowledge of the soul is obtained by reflection about our own thought. This is a turning inwards upon oneself, but, like all other forms of knowledge, it begins with sensory knowledge. Thomas brought this Aristotelian view of knowledge to its highest point in his ultimate appraisal of knowledge, which was also based on Aristotle's thought. Man's supreme ability is his capacity to think and his ultimate ideal lies in a knowledge of Truth, in other words, in beholding God, since even God as pure Act (*actus purus*) is, in the first place, a thinking of himself, a thinking of thinking, as Aristotle said, or Truth itself.

Man's second spiritual faculty is his will. Just as the intellect is of its very nature directed towards what is true, so is the will directed towards what is good. This does not mean, however, that the will is necessarily directed towards the highest good. It simply means that it can be directed towards something only if it regards this as a good. The will can therefore relinquish a deeper good for a momentary enjoyment. This possibility of choosing between various forms of good is what makes up man's freedom of choice. Even more fundamental than this freedom of choice, however, is the freedom that the will finds in aspiring towards its highest good. This supreme good is Goodness itself, in other words, God. It is in its orientation towards God that the human will finds its inner freedom. Freedom of choice is therefore only a way towards the realization of this inner freedom.

Thus the ultimate direction of the intellect and the will coincides. The will is seeking what is perfectly good and the intellect is seeking what is perfectly true and the perfectly Good and the perfectly True are simply different names for God. It is moreover the intellect which must inform the will as to what this perfect good is, since God is a spirit and can only be approached by the intellect and not by instinct or with the senses. On the other hand, however, it is the will which must maintain the intellect in its orientation towards God, because our senses and our desires are always trying to deflect this orientation.

It is therefore clear that man's participation in the divine Being is a participation of a very special kind. If the whole of creation is, by virtue of its being created by God, a participation in the divine Being, then this participation is for man on the one hand a point of departure and on the other a task. Since his intellect is directed towards truth and his will is directed towards goodness, then the more completely his intellect is directed towards truth and the more completely his will is directed towards goodness, the greater will be his participation in the divine Being. All truth and all goodness participate in the Truth and the Goodness of the divine Being.

This is the ultimate meaning of all scientific and moral aspiration and the positive appraisal of the terrestrial. The terrestrial has its own order. It is the task of science to know this and the task of morality to maintain it. Thus morality can be deducted from the way in which man was created by God, from his nature, and this applies to both individual and social morality, since man is by nature a social being. It is of the greatest importance to the ultimate individual aim of man, his vision of God, not only that his own individuality should be directed towards this end, but also that the whole of society should be ordered according to the demands of human nature, that is to say, that society should play its part in helping to subordinate all human desires to the intellect and the will. Moreover, no desire is in itself evil. On the contrary, every desire is in itself good. Desires can, however, be evil when they overstep the limits of their proper sphere and do not support the intellect and the will but deflect them from their fundamental orientation. The ideal of morality is therefore not to kill the passions, but to regulate them so that they may make a positive contribution to the realization of man's being.

Nonetheless, the possibility and even the day to day reality of evil remains. Very few men achieve the ideal regulation of human passions, intellect and will. What is this evil, if there is, as we have already seen, no principle of evil and if everything proceeds from God? Are we bound to say either that evil comes from God or that it has a being that is independent of God? Both of these solutions are unacceptable. Evil *is* not and consequently has no being that is independent of God as the Creator. Evil is simply the absence of good, of the good that ought to be present (*absentia boni debiti*). This applies to all evil, both physical evil (hardship, disease and so on) and moral evil, that is, sin.

If the reality of the created being is its participation in the being of the Creator, does it not therefore follow from this that we must know God directly and that our knowledge of God consequently must take place at least without the mediation of our senses? It does follow from the fact that the created being is a participation in the uncreated Being that this is the central point for metaphysical thought, but it does not follow that this is also the point of departure for knowing. We know our being first as a participation by reflection. Our first knowledge is a knowledge of the world of the senses and therefore a knowledge of ourselves as knowing. We first discover God when we seek an explanation for this world and for ourselves.

The ontological proof of the existence of God provided by St Anselm has to be rejected because it moves from the order of thought to the order of being in a manner that cannot be justified. A proof of the existence of God can only be *a posteriori*. Thomas therefore provides five proofs. Movement in the world means that we must accept the existence of a first unmoved Mover. Since everything must have a cause, but since nothing can be explained by going on indefinitely, there must be a first uncaused Cause. Since the contingent things of the world do not explain themselves, there must also be a necessary Being to which these contingent things owe their existence. Since there are degrees of perfection in all finite beings, there must also be an infinitely perfect Being which is the cause of all finite perfections. Finally, there is purpose in the universe and this presupposes that the universe must be regulated by an Intellect that is distinct from the universe.

Thomas also maintained with the greatest insistence that, although we can certainly demonstrate that there is a Being that causes everything and exists in itself, we cannot know the distinctive nature of this Being that we call God. We certainly know *that* God is, but we do not know *what* he is. All the same, it is possible to speak of a certain philosophical knowledge of God and we can do this on the basis of the theory of participation. In this, Thomas faithfully followed the Pseudo-Dionysius, but was at the same time able to harmonize the neo-Platonism of the Pseudo-Dionysius with his own Aristotelian theory of knowledge. This he did in the following way. Since all created being is to some extent a participation in the uncreated Being, all the positive good in creatures can be attributed to the Creator (*via positiva*). On the other hand, however, it is clear—by reason of the analogy of being, which means that there is similarity and difference in the same—that every created perfection as created and limited must be denied of God (*via negativa*). This means therefore that the created good is present in God in a way which completely surpasses this created good, just as the Creator infinitely surpasses the creature (*via eminentiae*).

This, then, is the Thomist synthesis in its broad outlines. It was the product of continuous controversy. On the one hand, he was in constant conflict with the thinkers of the neo-Platonic school, who were very eclectic in their use of Aristotle. On the other hand, he would not, as a Christian, accept any interpretation of Aristotle which was contradictory to faith. Nonetheless, after Thomas's death, in 1277, Etienne Tempier, the Bishop of Paris, condemned some of Thomas's theses and the Archbishops of Canterbury, the Dominican Robert Kilwardby and later the Franciscan John Peckham, supported this condemnation. All the same, Thomas's views were defended from the very outset by enthusiastic disciples. Albert the Great took up the cudgels on his behalf and the magisters of the Dominican order were gradually won over to Thomism. The magisters of the Franciscan order, however, remained faithful to the traditional views and those of the other orders and among the secular clergy were divided in their opinions about Thomism. When Thomas was canonized in 1323, the condemnations were finally revoked.

The danger on the Aristotelian side that Thomas had to combat was above all Averroism, the interpretation of Aristotle made by the greatest of his Arabic commentators, Averroes. The most important protagonist of this interpretation in the second half of the thirteenth century was SIGER OF BRABANT, a canon at Liège and a magister in the faculty of liberal arts at Paris. It is unfortunately very difficult to provide a really faithful rendering of Siger's views, since his thought shows a distinct development; his writings have only been published in part and there are still many unsettled questions concerning the dates and the authenticity of his works.

In his early period, Siger defended the view that there was only one intellect which did not form a substantial unity with the human soul, but was only concerned with it in a working unity (monopsychism). Later, however, under the influence of Thomas, Siger changed his view to some extent. He continued to maintain, with numerous arguments, that there was only one intellect, but at the same time opposed these arguments with many counter-statements which made this teaching difficult to uphold. His conclusion in a case of doubt of this kind, was that it was best to rely on faith. Thomas's arguments for the individuality of the human intellect had their effect on him, however, and forced Siger to seek a more satisfactory solution. He was eventually led to admit that the fact that the individual human being was able to understand could not be explained by a working unity between the intellect and the human soul. For this, a substantial unity between the intellect and the soul was necessary. Thus Siger came to abandon the monopsychism of Averroes, although he continued to declare that, in spite of everything, Averroes' view had great probability. This deductive probability, however, was, in Siger's opinion, contrary to the experience of the psychic life and was therefore not based on truth.

Although this was the central issue at stake in the controversy between Siger and Thomas, there were other related bones of contention. Thus Siger believed that it could be proved by thought that the world did not have a beginning, although faith taught that the world did have a beginning. This, of course, at once gives rise to a conflict with faith similar to that found in the doctrine of monopsychism, and Siger consequently stressed again and again that, even when philosophy could come to no other than one conclusion, faith nonetheless could teach that the reality was different. This view was later given the name of the doctrine of double truth, but it is doubtful whether this name really reflects Siger's intention. This is even more difficult to establish because it is never entirely clear whether Siger was speaking here on his own account or simply as an interpreter of Aristotle.

But, despite the condemnations issued by the Bishop of Paris in 1270 and 1277, Siger's Averroism apparently continued to make itself felt in the faculty of liberal arts. In the first quarter of the fourteenth century, the doctrine of double truth was maintained without any reservations at all in the work of certain thinkers. In several cases, philosophy led to completely different results from those reached through faith. In these cases, both the statements of philosophy and those of faith were, despite their mutual contradiction, claimed as certain and true, since what was absurd to us was not, these thinkers maintained, necessarily absurd to God.

The influence of Albert the Great is strikingly apparent in the work of JOHN ECKHART, although this thinker, who was born in 1260 or thereabouts in Hochheim near Gotha, gave greater emphasis to neo-Platonic than to Aristotelian elements. After entering the Dominican order, it is probable that he studied first at Cologne and then in Paris. He taught in Paris from 1300 until 1302 and again from 1311 until 1314. In between these two periods and after 1314, he occupied high positions in his order and taught in Strasbourg and Cologne. His work, however, came to be viewed with suspicion and the Bishop of Cologne set up a commission in 1326 to investigate it. Meister Eckhart declared that he had no intention of teaching anything that was not in accordance with faith and, in 1327, appealed to the Pope. He died, however, the same year. In 1329, Pope John XXII condemned twenty-eight theses found in Eckhart's work by the Cologne commission. There can be no doubt about Eckhart's subjective orthodoxy. His objective orthodoxy, however, is still a controversial issue.

Eckhart was one of the first of the medieval thinkers to use his own language as well as Latin. His writings in Latin are certainly the most important as far as his philosophical ideas are concerned, but the difficulty is that they have not yet been published in full. These Latin writings are, however, supplemented by his writings in German. Just as some medieval thinkers tended to work within the framework of the natural sciences and others in the sphere of ontology, so too did Eckhart tend in a particular direction. His special contribution was his elaboration of Albert's and Thomas's thought on mysticism. His Latin treatises provide the theoretical and speculative substructure for his practical and mystical sermons in the vernacular. There is a very close connection between speculative and mystical thought in Eckhart.

Thomas's distinction between essence and existence played an important part both in the work of Eckhart and in that of AEGIDIUS ROMANUS, otherwise known as Giles of Rome (1247–1316). Aegidius argued that existence and essence were not only distinct, but even separable in a being. Eckhart, on the other hand, affirmed that every being had its own essence, but participated in God's existence, which was the only real existence. He thus took Thomas's distinction in a different direction from Aegidius, but both his and Aegidius's theories deviated from Thomas's original intention. If God is the existence of every being, there is nothing outside God. This makes a mystical union with God possible, a union which takes place not simply in the intellect (as Thomas maintained) and in love (as Bonaventure held), but in the deepest being of the soul itself (the ground or the spark of the soul). The manner in which Eckhart expressed these ideas shows a certain tendency towards pantheism, and it is still a matter of controversy to what extent Eckhart's manner of expressing himself arose from a need to communicate his experience of God in a vivid way or whether it really encroached upon his monotheistic thinking.

5. *The* Via Antiqua *and the* Via Moderna

Philosophy reached its highest point in the Middle Ages in the second half of the thirteenth century and the first quarter of the fourteenth century, after which a spirit which was distinctly averse from constructive philosophy gradually began to make itself felt. Even those who remained faithful to constructive thought tended to be inflexible. They grouped themselves into schools—the leading schools of Thomism and Scotism and the less influential schools of Augustinianism and Albertism—all of which showed the same lack of originality. They saw no way of extending or deepening their philosophical ideas with the help of criticism, but, in general, went no farther than their great predecessors had gone. The most interesting figures in this *via antiqua* are the mystics, who based their thought on traditional philosophy without in any way developing it as Eckhart, for example, had done. Any original contribution that they made was chiefly in the sphere of mystical theology.

JOHN RUYSBROECK (1293–1381), a chaplain at the St Goedele in Brussels, who, together with others of like mind, founded a monastery in 1343 in the Zonienbos, was, in his thought, very faithful to Augustinianism. All Ruysbroeck's works had an essentially practical origin—he was aware of the need to combat certain heretical trends in mysticism not simply negatively, but by a positive mysticism. It was for this reason too that Ruysbroeck wrote all his works in the vernacular. Ruysbroeck had no interest in purely philosophical questions. Unlike Eckhart, he never mixed in philosophical circles and never taught in centres of philosophy. But, needing a philosophy on which to base his mystical theology, he chose traditional neo-Platonic Augustinianism, probably because he had himself been brought up in this school of thought and partly perhaps because it was not a controversial issue. Thus, at least in the Netherlands, the Augustinian movement continued to exist outside the conflict between the various schools.

Like all mystics, Ruysbroeck was principally interested in man's union with God and in his work he again and again described the ascent of man towards the vision of God. Although he emphasized man's necessary activity in this, he at the same time stressed that this ascent was not within man's own power. As it meant a divinization of man, it could only by achieved by God. Man, however, had to purify himself in order to be receptive to God's action. The union between man and God came about in this way, but Ruysbroeck insisted that this union was never identity—the infinite distance between the Creator and the creature was always preserved even when the creature lost consciousness of his own life. The ascent to God was a laborious journey because it was impossible to grasp God's being in a purely human manner. In Ruysbroeck's view, if man wished to ascend to God, he had to hold himself aloof from his own human way of seeing, thinking and willing.

It was only in this way, Ruysbroeck believed, that God's image could be formed in man. His mysticism was, like Eckhart's, strongly influenced by the thought of the Pseudo-Dionysius. But he was more careful than Eckhart, whom he occasionally attacked indirectly, not to allow this Pseudo-Dionysian influence to result in pantheism.

Another thinker who was also influenced by this movement was DIONYSIUS OF RIJCKEL (1402–71), who, after having studied in Cologne, became a Carthusian at Roermond. Like his friend, Nicholas of Cusa, Dionysius was intensely preoccupied with the religious and political problems of his period. He still, however, found time for intense literary activity in the sphere of philosophy, theology and mysticism. It is clear from his writings that he was familiar with the great scholastics of the High Middle Ages, with the work of John Ruysbroeck and with the whole thought of the fourteenth century. His point of departure was Thomist.

Like Ruysbroeck, Dionysius was mainly concerned with man's ascent to God. His thought can be briefly summarized as follows. Although the senses are absolutely necessary for man's knowledge of the things of this world, the soul can only come to a knowledge of God and of itself by reflecting about itself. The beatific vision ultimately excludes the whole of the created world. It sees God as existing—*quia est,* and it sees his being—*quid est.* But it grasps his being only in a negative manner, because it clearly comprehends that God is absolutely incomprehensible. Together with the thought of Nicholas of

Cusa, that of Dionysius was the most constructive of the fifteenth century and, because he had an extensive knowledge of the work of his predecessors and was able to express their thought accurately, he performed a special service in handing down the great systems of scholastic thought to the centuries that followed.

The *via moderna* was in several respects different from the great scholastic systems and from the *via antiqua*. In the first place, it tended to reject constructive metaphysics and to concentrate more on the human manner of knowing than on the being of beings. Secondly, its doctrine of knowing, whether it went back emphatically to the problems of the *universalia* of the beginning of the twelfth century or not, certainly followed a nominalist tendency. Finally, the *via moderna* was just as interested in positively scientific problems as in purely philosophical questions, or even more so. It would not be true to say that the *via moderna* was less interested in theology than the *via antiqua*, but we can certainly say that the theology of this school was very much concerned with the concrete problems of political life and the life of the Church. Although Ockham was its most representative thinker, the *via moderna* did not begin with him. The principle that beings must not be multiplied without reason—*entia non sunt sine ratione multi-plicanda*—is older than Ockham, although it is famous as 'Ockham's razor'.

The Franciscan WILLIAM OF OCKHAM (*c.* 1290–1350) studied and taught at Oxford. In 1324, he had to defend his theses at the papal court at Avignon. They were not condemned. In 1328, William took sides against Pope John XXII and fled to the court of Emperor Ludwig of Bavaria. From that moment onwards, he was involved in the religious and political struggles of his time and his numerous writings show that he violently opposed the power of the Pope and firmly supported the supreme power of the state. Much of what he wrote at this period had a great influence on the quarrel between the Emperor and the Pope. In these writings, he discussed such political questions as national sovereignty and the relationship between Church and state and this led to the emergence of a new political science which was fully developed in the Renaissance, especially by Machiavelli.

Ockham, clearly influenced by Duns Scotus, took the individuality of each being as his starting point. The individual being, he maintained, has nothing in common with any other individual being whatever. The universal therefore does not exist in any way in the nature of things, but only in the intellect. Furthermore, only real distinctions, that is, distinctions between what is really separable, are meaningful. Ockham thus denied the existence of a number of traditional distinctions, such as that between essence and existence, which, because they were not really separable, were, in his opinion, only two different ways of looking at the same reality. The same applied, he believed, to quantity, which could not be separated from the material thing, with the result that quantity and matter were, in his opinion, also identical. There is also no reality in any relationship outside its terms. The relationship is simply a concept. Since there is no other reality apart from that of the individual, the most important form of knowledge is that which is empirical or intuitive and attuned to the individual. This intuitive knowledge is twofold. It is sensory and intellectual. These two aspects of knowledge always go together. Abstract knowledge is possible because of the intellectual element which can form a universal concept that is only a sign or a name (*nomen*) for several individual things— hence the term nominalism.

The consequence of this is that all metaphysical concepts have only a subjective meaning and that there is therefore no certain knowledge of God or the soul. Only faith can give any certainty here. Ockham also maintained that the essence of the soul and of God was to be found in the human and the divine will. It is therefore God's will which established creation and the order of creation. Everything that is created is absolutely contingent and we can only trace, in this contingent creation, the accidental order which can be arbitrarily changed by God. The moral order therefore depends entirely on God's arbitrary will. There are no moral norms fully valid in themselves.

Ockhamism spread rapidly throughout Europe. It soon became the leading movement in Oxford and in Paris it gained many supporters and occupied an important place beside the *via antiqua*. It also found favour in Germany and Italy. The University of Louvain, however, which was founded in 1425, rejected Ockhamism from the beginning. Round about the middle of the fourteenth century, the *via moderna* flourished in Paris.

The clearest proof of the ability of the nominalist doctrine to achieve full reconciliation with Christian theology and practice is to be found in the works of the two Frenchmen, Peter d'Ailly and John Gerson. PETER D'AILLY (1350–1420), the Bishop of Cambrai and a Cardinal, played a leading part in reforming the Church of his time. Philosophically, he was opposed to Aristotelianism and a fairly radical Ockhamist. He was convinced that no more than probability could be attained in metaphysical matters, that God's existence and the existence of the outside world could not be proved beyond all doubt and that the natural and the moral order were entirely dependent on God's will. JOHN GERSON (1363–1429), who succeeded d'Ailly as the Chancellor of the University of Paris, was a theologian and a philosopher, but above all a mystic. Although he limited the frontiers of natural knowledge very severely, he nonetheless upheld the validity of metaphysical arguments. He was clearly afraid that nominalism would, if it was carried too far, lead to scepticism, and consequently quite often followed the *via antiqua*. He maintained firmly that our concepts were related to an objective reality. He was also afraid of the danger of pantheism in Ruysbroeck.

With the emergence of humanism, nominalism quickly lost ground. The logical hair-splitting, which it had by this time largely become, was unable to withstand the mockery of the humanists. The critical spirit of the nominalists and their respect for and interest in positive science, however, continued to have an effect and influenced the earliest thinkers of the modern age. But, in the meantime, humanism was already beginning to play an important part in philosophy. As early as the fifteenth century, philosophy was being practised in Italy in a completely unscholastic manner. Between scholasticism and humanism, however, there was the highly original thought of Nicholas of Cusa.

NICHOLAS OF CUSA, who was born in 1401 at Cusa near Trèves, was educated first by the Brothers of the Common Life at Deventer and then at the Universities of Heidelberg, Padua and Cologne, where he was brought into contact with the important philosophical and theological movements of the time. He soon became involved in the religious and political struggles of the period and was given important tasks by the Pope. He became a Cardinal in 1448 and was made Bishop of Brixen in 1450. He died at Trodi in 1464. Despite constant activity in the Church, he managed to write a great deal. His Treatises, most of which were written in Latin, although some were in German, covered many different spheres of knowledge, including mathematics, natural science, astronomy, philosophy, theology and mysticism. His most important work was *De docta ignorantia* (1440). It is in this theme of 'knowing ignorance' that the essence of his philosophy is to be found.

There are, he said, three modes of knowing. We know material things through our senses. On the basis of this sensory knowledge, our reason forms abstract concepts in accordance with the principle of contradiction. Knowledge is limited and relative because things are individual. Unlimited and perfect knowledge is to be found only in God, from whom all things proceed. Nonetheless, there is a higher knowledge to which man can attain by intuition. The principle of contradiction does not apply to intuition, which is capable of grasping the unity of the opposites that cannot be resolved by man's reason. It is therefore wisdom to be conscious of the ignorance in which reason leaves us. This ignorance is the point of departure for intuition and through it we can attain to the reality in which all contradiction is resolved. That reality is God.

God is the unity of opposites—he is at the same time the greatest and the smallest being, existence and non-existence. No comparison is possible between divine transcendence and the finite being. We can speak of more or less only in the case of finite beings, but their existence is like a non-existence as compared with God. God therefore transcends all the contradictions that we encounter in the finite sphere. Our knowledge of God consequently consists of statements of what he is not (the *via negativa*) and of statements of what he is (the *via positiva*), which cancel each other out, but which also, in their mutual relationships, point to the perfectly transcendent One. This perfect transcendence is unknowable to us. We are, however, able to make imperfect statements about him because of his relationships with the world.

As the infinite One, God is everything that can be. Everything is in him and he is in everything. This does not, however, imply pantheism—we necessarily express ourselves in human words, but God transcends the contrasts which we express in words and does so in a manner which escapes human reason. God is therefore not identical with the universe. The principle of the identity of opposites applies to God, but not to the Creator in his relationships with creation. Created things are multiform images of God called into existence by God. They belong to different spheres—sensual, rational and spiritual—but these three spheres are always occurring in different combinations. There are traces of the spirit everywhere, but nothing is without sensuality. Man is a unity of the three spheres, the centre of creation and the most perfect image of God—he is the microcosm. His soul is immortal and is accidentally united with his body.

The whole world returns to God, for whom it is created. This return is motivated by love. Every being strives towards perfection and man does this by knowing and willing. His spiritual nature enables him to approach God intimately and the multiformity of his being achieves unity in this approach. This unity reaches its climax in spiritual intuition, in which even the principle of contradiction, as we have seen, no longer applies. As a Christian, Nicholas of Cusa insisted that this return to God was only possible for man through Christ.

Nicholas summed up the whole of medieval thought in one last great synthesis. Many different influences contributed to the originality of his mind—Augustine and the Pseudo-Dionysius, John Scotus Eriugena and Anselm, the great figures of the scholasticism of the High Middle Ages and of nominalism, the mysticism of the Netherlands and the Rhineland and Averroism. But, much more than the synthesis of his friend Dionysius, his synthesis also pointed to the future. It contained much of the thought of the humanists and his interest in positive science makes him part of the great tradition leading from Roger Bacon and Albert the Great via many others to modern scientific thought. The unity which was always present in Nicholas's mind was unity in Christ. He saw Christ not only as the centre of all scientific thought, but also as the centre of all social life. It is in this light that his striving towards religious and social unity must be seen. This was expressed above all in his first work, but it also played a very powerful part in his later writings and especially in his practical activities. There is evidence of this, for example, in his unceasing work for the reunion of Eastern and Western Christianity and the conversion of the Mohammedans. With the aim of converting Islam, he was the first western thinker to approach the Koran scientifically.

He was open to the thought of the humanists. His first scientific action was his discovery of a manuscript of Plautus. He had contacts with various Greeks who had settled in Italy and were working zealously there for a more profound study of Plato.

The influence of the Greeks on thought became much greater at this time, especially as many Greeks sought refuge in Italy after the fall of Constantinople in 1453. The complete translation of Plato and Plotinus at this time made it possible to distinguish clearly between Platonism and neo-Platonism. Humanism was clearly revealed in the work of JOHN PICO DELLA MIRANDOLA (1463–94), whose *De dignitate hominis* presented the central theme of humanism, as this prevailed in the Platonic Academy of Florence. It is both here and in the work of Nicholas of Cusa that modern thought was most clearly heralded in the fifteenth century.

3 The Formation of Modern Philosophy

1. *The Philosophy of the Renaissance*

The period of the fifteenth and sixteenth centuries has a special significance in the development of European man. Much more than at any time in the previous history of man, thought was directed in the Renaissance towards man's individuality. The medieval idea of the correlation of the individual and the community—the individual and the community existing in a necessary and mutual relationship—was replaced by a vision of man which regarded the community only as a means towards the development of the individual. This development was intimately connected with the vigorous self-confidence that characterized Renaissance man. The two feelings of freedom and self-confidence led in many respects to an essential deepening of thought and experience, but at the same time to uncontrollable tensions which became more powerful with the passing of time. Simultaneously, the natural sciences began to find their own methods and gradually to become dissociated from philosophy. Philosophy quickly reacted to this dissociation by reflecting more deeply about its own nature and in turn dissociating itself from its bonds with theology, which resulted in a deeper reflection about the true nature of philosophy as distinct from that of theology. A renewed study of ancient philosophy played a special part in this. Despite all this, however, the centuries of the Renaissance were not directly fruitful for the development of philosophy and it was not until the seventeenth century that the powerful feeling for life that characterized this period found adequate philosophical expression.

Although the revival of Platonism and Stoicism was very important in the sixteenth century, the resurgence of natural science on the one hand and of political science on the other contributed far more to the development of philosophy in the centuries that followed. Predominant for almost all the thinkers who broke away from scholasticism, were either problems of natural science or questions about the nature of the state. Here too, however, it was not until the seventeenth century that any clear answer was found to these questions, when, in the first half of that century, Hugo Grotius provided a firm basis for the Renaissance ideas of the state and the community of nations, while Galileo clearly pointed out the way along which natural science should develop.

Far more than in the Middle Ages, the philosophy of the Renaissance contained a pronounced element of magic. The many new discoveries in the field of natural science and man's growing knowledge of the earth and its peoples led to imagination running riot and magic played a great part in this. For a time, it was easier to conceive all these new discoveries imaginatively, in magic images, than in rational thought. This magical thought reached a remarkable climax in the writings of the German PARACELSUS (1493–1541), who combined in a highly capricious manner natural science, magical imagination, medicine and quackery. This magical element was as much a characteristic of Renaissance thought as were both serious reflection about politics and the growth of natural science with its emphasis on unprejudiced perception.

Italy and Germany produced the most important figures in the field of thought about nature at this time. LEONARDO DA VINCI (1452–1519) clearly understood that nature could only be known by experience and that, in order to practise natural science, this experience had to be gained by experiment and worked out along mathematical lines. In his methodical matter-of-factness and his aversion from all speculative thought about nature, he anticipated Galileo and had no parallel until Galileo. Because his work remained unknown, however, the ideas that were contained in it had no influence on his contemporaries or on later thinkers. NICHOLAS COPERNICUS (Thorn, Poland, 1473–Frauenburg, East Prussia, 1543), who studied for some time in Italy, published the thesis that the sun did not revolve around the earth, but that the earth revolved around the sun. This not only undermined the foundations of Aristotelian physics on which man's idea of the universe had hitherto rested, but also prepared the way for a change in thought about the relationship between man and the universe.

The new idea of the world of the Renaissance was most vividly expressed by GIORDANO BRUNO. Born in 1548 at Nola in Campania, Bruno at a very early age became a Dominican, but both his thought and his way of life made it impossible for him to remain in the monastery. From 1576 onwards, he wandered through France, England and Germany before ultimately returning to Italy where he was accused of heresy, imprisoned in 1592 and finally burnt publicly in Rome in 1600, after having refused to revoke his teaching. Bruno was a fertile, but careless and unsystematic writer. Very many influences acted on him—Thomism (from his monastic training with the Dominicans), Averroism, the dialectics of Lull, Nicholas of Cusa, Copernicus, the magic ideas of Paracelsus, the natural philosophy of the Renaissance and finally ancient philosophy with which he was familiar through direct study. Bruno's natural scientific knowledge was not great and his philosophical pronouncements were not consistent.

His philosophical thought moved between two opposite poles—on the one hand, the one, infinite universe and, on the other hand, God, the Creator of this universe. The tensions between these two poles were such that the universe was seen as the creation of God who was himself above it, while the universe was also seen as an expression of God which was, in the last resort, God himself. Bruno did not work out either of these two possibilities consistently, but hovered between theism and pantheism without ever resolving this inward contradiction in his work. The universe consisted, in his view, of an infinite number of worlds which together formed one real unity. It was, so to speak, a living unity, an immense living being that was the perfect expression of God. He called man a 'monad' in which both the universe and God were reflected. Although he often allowed his imagination to run riot, Bruno undoubtedly saw the question of the close bond between God, the universe and man very clearly and felt it very intensely. His ideas were expressed in works written in both Latin and Italian and the title of one of his works is very characteristic— *Degli eroici furori,* 'On the Heroic Passions'.

TOMMASO CAMPANELLA (Stilo in Calabria, 1568–Paris, 1639) was, like Bruno, a Dominican. Taking the study of nature as his starting-point, he aimed to build up a complete metaphysics. He believed that nature could only be known through perception—his *Apologia pro Galileo* testifies to this. But, despite his obvious powers of observation and in contradiction to his principle, he often sought refuge in imagination in his explanation of the facts. For a firm point of departure in his theory of knowledge, he chose the testimony of consciousness. The further extension of our knowledge took place, in his view, along two ways. We come to know individual things by sensory perception. Discursive thought enables us to reach a more general knowledge, but it is a less sure way and this general knowledge is consequently more vague. The universe is 'the mirror in which the face of God is reflected', the perfect image of God. This universe is entirely inspired, like all separate things. This provided the basis for the study of astrology and magic, in which Tommaso, in common with most other Renaissance thinkers, had a great interest.

In the meantime, Copernicus' idea was further elaborated by JOHN KEPLER (1571–1630), although Galileo must be given credit for being the first man to have clearly defined and consistently applied the scientific method. GALILEO GALILEI was born in Pisa in 1564. The publication of his *Nuncius Sidereus* (1610), in which he defended Copernicus' system, led to a conflict with ecclesiastical authority. There was, however, no trial until he published, in 1632, his *Dialogo sopra i due massimi sistemi del mondo*. In this, he contrasted the ideas of Aristotle with those of Copernicus and came out strongly in favour of the latter. Copernicus' system was regarded as conflicting with Scripture and, as a result, Galileo was obliged to renounce his theses. He died at Florence in 1642.

Galileo's real significance is to be found less in his struggle to uphold and promote the Copernican view of the world, which he conducted rather inconsistently, than in the great consistency with which he applied the mathematical method in the field of natural science. For him, only perception and what could be deduced mathematically from this perception were of importance. With this method, he achieved important results in the field of astronomy and established the science of mechanics. He formulated and proved experimentally the first laws of natural science in the modern sense. He rejected the use of the imagination which had, despite many correct intuitions on the part of Italian and German Renaissance thinkers, again and again cut across the findings of experience. This does not mean, however, that experience was all that mattered to Galileo. Philosophy also played a considerable part in the working out of his ideas. He applied, for example, the time-honoured principle that nature always and necessarily acted in the simplest way and accepted the Platonic idea that the laws of nature were of a mathematical kind. With Galileo, natural science was finally dissociated from philosophy and made autonomous. This also made it possible for the method of natural science to be regarded as the scientific method *par excellence* and for everything that could not be achieved by this method to be regarded as unreal.

From the fifteenth century onwards, a new tradition came about, in addition to that of the natural scientists—a tradition of philosophers who, inspired by the confused and rapidly changing political situation of their own times, were principally concerned with political science. This tradition began with the Italian NICCOLÒ MACHIAVELLI (1467–1525) who, in his *Il Principe* (1513), advocated an autocratic form of government as the only solution to the prevailing political chaos. As this form of government was ultimately the only one that could, in Machiavelli's view, guarantee the well-being of the state, everything was permitted to the autocratic prince to maintain and strengthen his autocracy.

A new literary genre was created by the Englishman THOMAS MORE (1480–1535) who, in his *Utopia* (*De optimo reipublicae statu deque nova insula Utopia*, 1516), gave a picture of the ideal state which was, in More's book, to be found on a lonely island. Private ownership was unknown in Utopia, the state cared for everyone who rendered equivalent service by his work and the inhabitants of the island were averse from war and enjoyed complete religious freedom. The Utopian state was founded on complete equality. The Spaniard JUAN LUIS VIVES (1492–1540), who spent most of his life in England and Flanders, wrote, among other things, about international order. In addition to this, his educational works are particularly important. These even contain some of the rudiments of experimental psychology. The Frenchman JEAN BODIN (1530–97) was opposed to Utopian fantasies and believed that any philosophy of the state should draw its inspiration from a study of the history of political institutions. He pleaded power-fully in defence of the sovereignty of the state and, like the other thinkers mentioned here, argued that the state should not take up its stand on the basis of a particular religion. In his view, subjects were known to the state only as citizens, who should all be equal in the eyes of the state.

Tommaso Campanella (see above) was also concerned with questions of political philosophy. In his *Civitas solis* (*The City of the Sun*), he described the ideal state as a community governed according to the Platonic conception, in which the authority of the state was absolute and communal ownership prevailed. Much later, in his *De monarchia hispanica,* he was concerned with international order between the states, all or which were, in his book, subject to a higher authority, so as to avoid insoluble conflicts resulting from their autonomy. This higher authority was the pope, but, as the pope was without adequate worldly power, the task was undertaken on his behalf by the monarchy of Spain, the most powerful state at the beginning of the seventeenth century.

The idea of an international law reached its climax in a book by HUGO GROTIUS (1583–1645), *De iure belli ac pacis* (1625). Grotius based his views on the distinction that had been recognized by the Romans—that between natural law (*ius naturale*) and the law instituted by the state (*ius civile*). Natural law is the law that results from man's social nature and it applies to all men in all parts of the world and in all periods or history. It forms the juridical basis for relationships between individuals, between the individual and the state and between states. The basic rule of natural law, *pacta sunt servanda* (treaties must be honoured), applies to all relations between states. The idea of treaty also plays a part in the relationship between individuals and the state. By treaty, individuals have handed over some of their rights to the state, in order better to safe-guard their interests. In any study of the natural law, it is necessary to ascertain what rights the individual has transferred to the state and how the state must be equipped to safeguard these rights. The law of the state must never be allowed to come into conflict with the natural law. It must determine those concrete laws which will as far as possible fully guarantee that the natural law will be observed in the concrete circumstances of time and place.

Despite these three new philosophical tendencies which were so characteristic of the Renaissance—the renewed interpretation of the ancient philosophers, natural philosophy and political philosophy—scholasticism continued in the so-called post-scholastic school and nominalists, Thomists and Scotists remained active. Of these, Thomism was by far the most active. The Dominican, THOMAS DE VIO (1468–1534), who was known as CAJETAN after his birthplace, Gaeta, wrote commentaries on the works of Aristotle and Thomas Aquinas and a number of smaller works. He was, however, not simply a commentator, but a man of independent mind who made his own important contributions to such questions as that of analogy. He was also very interested in social and economic questions. He became a cardinal in 1517 and the second half of his life was almost entirely taken up with attempts to preserve the unity of the Church.

A very different figure from this Italian Dominican was the Spaniard FRANCIS OF VITORIA (1480–1556), also a Dominican, who did pioneering work in the field of international law in his book *Relectio de Indis* and who may be regarded as a predecessor of Hugo Grotius. Among other things, he rejected the idea of colonization. He was also the first man in the modern period to have proposed the theory of treaty as an explanation of the origin and validity of the ordering of the state. The philosophy of politics and law is the branch of philosophy in which post-scholasticism carried out its most original work.

Post-scholasticism reached its zenith in the work of the Spanish Jesuit, FRANCIS SUÁREZ (1548–1617). Suárez had a very great knowledge of the whole of scholasticism, of humanism and of the positive sciences. His *Disputationes metaphysicae* influenced not only subsequent scholastic thinking, but also modern philosophy. He too was deeply concerned with the natural law and international law.

The influence of post-scholasticism, which flourished mainly in Italy, Spain and Portugal, was quite considerable and was also felt for some time in other countries, in the sphere of university teaching. Germany and the Netherlands were especially influenced. The works of Suárez in particular were studied in these countries and, despite Luther's aversion from philosophy, a Protestant scholastic movement soon came into being alongside the Catholic scholastic tradition. The foundations of this Protestant scholasticism were laid by PHILIP MELANCHTHON (1497–1565), but the movement never became so important philosophically as the Protestant mysticism which flourished especially in Germany and reached its highest point in JAKOB BÖHME (1575–1624).

Two different influences are clearly discernible in the work of Böhme—that of Paracelsian magic thought and that of the German mystical tradition (Eckhart). How Böhme, who was not a scholar in the formal sense, but a simple shoemaker, ever came to these ideas is unknown. He had to endure a great deal of persecution because of his ideas, but, on the other hand, he also had very many supporters. He set out his ideas in numerous writings. Böhme saw reality as an all-embracing harmony, all being forming a unity which was immanently inspired by God. God was therefore, in Böhme's view, one with this reality and did not transcend it. A problem was raised by the presence of evil, but Böhme saw this too as being within the all-embracing reality and as necessary, as the negative aspect, for the disclosure of the positive aspect of this reality. For him, all being

E

contained, within its unity, the contrast between the positive and the negative aspects of reality, between good and evil. In this way, reality was in continuous motion and man, in whom the struggle took place, participated in this movement.

Although MICHEL DE MONTAIGNE (1533–92) did not consider himself to be a philosopher, he to a very great extent prepared the way for the heyday of French philosophy in the seventeenth century and to some extent too laid the foundations for the whole of modern French philosophy. He completely broke with scholastic thought, which he regarded as degenerate in its hair-splitting arguments about unimportant problems. He tried to find his own way in the confusion of ideas at the time. In his *Essais*, he did not provide a systematic philosophy, but simply wrote down the thoughts that occurred to him as a result of the most divergent circumstances. His own self was the centre of his interest, but from a consideration of himself he moved out to consider a number of important problems. He was also opposed to any unreflecting acceptance of prevailing ideas and to hasty solutions, and the weapon that he used was doubt. But, although he doubted everything, he was unable to find conclusive arguments for these doubts. He justified this scepticism by appealing to the obvious antithesis between the results of intellectual knowledge on the one hand and those of the knowledge of the senses on the other. These themes—of the subject 'I', of doubt and of the contrast between the two modes of knowledge—recurred both in Descartes and in Pascal.

Philosophy flourished in the seventeenth century, and the way was undoubtedly prepared not only by the scepticism of Montaigne, but also by the empiricism of FRANCIS BACON (1561–1626). Bacon tried, on the one hand, to find an explanation for the very limited progress of science and, on the other, to indicate how science could be practised more fruitfully. Man was, Bacon claimed, led astray in his practice of science by four kinds of illusion, which he called *idola—idola tribus* (the idols of the tribe, in other words, of the whole human race), which caused man to regard the things of nature as something human, *idola specus* (the idols of the den), which caused man to remain a captive in his own ideas as though in a den, *idola fori* (the idols of the market-place), which made man cling without reflecting to general statement and *idola theatri* (the idols of the stage), which made man invest one particular philosophical system with absolute authority. Bacon's positive achievement was to emphasize that true scientific results could only be attained by observation, experiment and setting the facts in order. He did not, however, advance science in any way himself and even appears to have been badly informed about what had already been achieved in his own time. His greatest importance was certainly in his critical awareness and his outlining of guiding principles. In this, he exercised a powerful influence on later English philosophy.

The points of departure for the synthetic thought of the seventeenth century were thus provided by Montaigne and Bacon—on the one hand, attention focussed on man and, on the other, on the world. Montaigne was concerned with the inward aspect of man as formed in a world of men, whereas Bacon concentrated his gaze on the world, at the same time showing that the inward aspect was of importance if this vision was to be correct.

2. *The Formation of the Basic Ideas*

In the seventeenth century, the thought of the Renaissance achieved maturity and fulfilment in the work of a number of great philosophers. In these cases, philosophical thought was no longer a rather arbitrary fusion of elements of scholastic philosophy and the positive sciences, but a complete unity which acted as a constant inspiration to the centuries that followed.

Later thought was influenced more by Descartes than by any other seventeenth-century philosopher. RENÉ DESCARTES, who was born in 1596 at La Haye in Touraine, received a scholastic education, but this gave him so little satisfaction that he decided to leave book-learning and consult the book of life. He found peace and an atmosphere in which he could work undisturbed in the Netherlands, where he remained for twenty years, eventually leaving to go to the court of Queen Christina of Sweden, where he died within a year, in 1650. He published comparatively few works—*Discours de la méthode de bien conduire sa raison et chercher la vérité dans les sciences* (the six-part *Discourse*, 1637), *Meditationes de prima philosophia* (*Meditations on First Philosophy*, 1641), *Principia philosophiae* (*Principles of Philosophy*, 1644), which was intended as an educational manual, and *Traités des passions de l'âme* (*Passions of the Soul*, 1649).

Descartes was affected by the uncertainty that prevailed in the thought of his time. Late scholasticism was unable to deal with the results of the positive sciences and the many and mutually contradictory forms of Renaissance philosophy were unsuccessful in their attempts to fit these results into a philosophical framework. Whereas the authority of Aristotle had an inhibiting effect on late scholasticism, imagination was allowed to run riot in the philosophy of Descartes's contemporaries. There seemed to Descartes to be no other course but to make a complete break with all the philosophical ideas that he encountered in traditional philosophy and in his own period and make a completely new beginning. To make a new beginning and at the same time to work methodically, however, required a firm point of departure and Descartes saw the solution to this problem in doubt. But anything that is open to doubt cannot form an unshakeable point of departure. If, however, I carry my doubt on with extreme consistency, I will ultimately encounter an indubitable truth, namely that I think. Doubting is itself also thinking. But, if I think, I also exist—*cogito ergo sum*. Existence is therefore discovered with and in thought.

Descartes's doubt was not doubting in order to doubt, but doubting in order to find the truth, of whose existence he was absolutely convinced. His doubt was therefore only a methodical doubt which is undertaken to keep us from building our philosophical house on unsound foundations. It is thus a question of coming to justified conclusions from this point of departure of doubt. But how can we guarantee that we shall not once again slip into our old prejudices on the way from this point of departure to the ultimate conclusion? There is only one way of avoiding this trap—the same thinking that enables us to find a firm point of departure must also have exclusive control over the drawing of conclusions from this point of departure. Thus, the only certain conclusion that can be drawn is the one that can be expressed in clear and distinct ideas (*idées claires et distinctes*). Anything that cannot be expressed in this way does not concern philosophy. Since mathematics always works with precisely defined points of departure and with conclusions expressed in clear and distinct ideas, it is the model for philosophical thought.

Thinking in clear and distinct ideas demands first of all the division of reality into two irreducible spheres—consciousness, which is essentially thought, and matter, which is essentially extension. Consciousness is only known in inner experience and extension is only known by mathematics. In material things, therefore, only that which can be counted or measured mathematically has reality. In consciousness, on the other hand, only that which can be clearly and distinctly identified by thought has reality. This division of reality into two spheres is of fundamental importance to the consideration of man, who, in this light, appears also as an irreducible duality—consciousness, soul, thought on the one hand and matter, body, extension on the other. There does, however, appear to be some kind of incomprehensible interaction between the two parts of this irreducible duality, each of which is, in itself, an independent unit or 'substance'. Descartes struggled with this problem throughout the whole of his life without being able to clarify it. Only thought can lead us to true knowledge, he believed, because it is in thought that we discover our innate concepts. The knowledge of the senses is, on the other hand, misleading.

Freedom is an inherent characteristic of the thinking consciousness, whereas the body is essentially without freedom. Together with thought, freedom is the ornament of man. In itself, our freedom is no less than that of God. It is simply a question of realizing our freedom by controlling our passions or emotions. Descartes distinguished six fundamental passions from which the others could be deduced—admiration, love and hatred, desire, joy and grief. Whenever man controls these passions in his thought, freedom can take him farther than ever thought can take him. Then freedom is not dominated by any external power, but reigns itself in its sovereign decisions. In this sense, it is not subject to the limitation of our thought, which is always restricted to a narrow sphere. But, although freedom has this greatness, it can also be the cause of my mistakes, because I am easily led by my freedom to make statements in matters which lie outside the limits of my intellect.

The ultimate guarantee for my thinking and willing is God, through whom I have the certainty that I shall not be deceived in my innate ideas. His existence is as firmly established as my own, because the finite is only conceivable against the background of the infinite. All thought therefore includes a relationship with God. The concept of God is so clear in itself that it cannot be denied and his existence is already given with the concept of God (the ontological proof). Although the *cogito* forms the firm point of departure of thought, God forms the guarantee of the *cogito* and everything that proceeds from it. Otherwise, it would always be possible for me to be led astray by a malicious spirit.

Descartes provided modern thought with a definite direction and it is possible to understand both the idealism and the positivism of later periods in the light of Cartesian ideas. He also posed the problems with which philosophers are still struggling today. He did not do this, however, by breaking completely with traditional thought as he himself claimed. In various ways, both Augustine and Anselm strongly influenced his thinking.

A philosopher who violently opposed Descartes was PIERRE GASSENDI (1592–1655) who, like Descartes, abandoned Aristotelian physics for modern physics, but sought an entirely different basis for it, in the atomism of Epicurus. The Epicurean influence also dominated his ethical ideas. Gassendi rejected Descartes's dualism and his ontological proof of the existence of God.

BLAISE PASCAL (1623–62), who was a mathematician, a physicist and a philosopher, was a younger contemporary of Descartes. He never wrote a systematic philosophical work, although he did plan to publish a full defence of the Christian religion, his notes for which were published after his death under the title of the *Pensées*. Pascal shared Descartes's love of mathematics and physics and certainly surpassed Descartes in his understanding of the nature of physics. He accepted and applied Galileo's inductive experimental method, whereas Descartes simply put forward his own deductive method in opposition to the deductive method of the Middle Ages. Pascal did not, like Descartes, take mathematics as the model for the philosophical method. For him, philosophy had to be first and foremost concerned with the individual, concrete man. In the study of man, Pascal was convinced that the reality was essentially a mystery and that although our thinking could certainly provide us with an insight into this mystery, it could not grasp it in adequate concepts. The *esprit de géométrie* could not reveal anything of the deepest reality—only the *esprit de finesse* could do this.

For Pascal, man was not an irreducible duality, but a unity of opposites. He lives in a state of tension and, although this tension is constantly requiring man to make decisions, it is not cancelled out by any of these decisions. It is not simply the basic elements of the intellect that are involved in making these decisions—the deeper elements of the heart are also involved. The deepest decision is that in which man forgets the world, forgets everything except God. Pascal's philosophy is a dialogue between concrete man and God—man who is nothing in the universe, but who is, on the other hand, the only thing in the universe that thinks. It is therefore only man who can come into contact with God, but he can also turn away from God. The *Pensées* provide a concrete philosophy of man's relationship with God.

There is a threefold order in the human reality—the order of bodies, that of spirits and that of love. In the order of bodies, there are greater and smaller—one is richer or more powerful than another. But the greatest wealth or power is of no importance in the order of spirits. The rich and the powerful are not capable of recognizing greatness of the spirit, which is known only to those who live by the spirit. Archimedes is not recognized by those who live according to the body. Only those who live according to the spirit recognize his greatness. But greatness of the spirit is nothing in comparison with the greatness of love. The spirit is not capable of recognizing holiness, which is seen only by God himself and the angels. All bodies together are unable to produce a single thought, because thought belongs to a different order. All bodies and all spirits together are incapable of a single movement of true love, because love belongs to a higher, supernatural order.

Modern thinking has been far more essentially determined by the rationalism of Descartes than by Pascal's reverence for mystery. In contemporary philosophy, however, there is fairly general criticism of Descartes and growing interest in Pascal.

NICOLE MALEBRANCHE (1678–1715) to some extent provided a synthesis of the thought of Descartes and Pascal. His chief work was his *Entretiens sur la métaphysique et sur la religion* (1699). He was strongly influenced by Augustine. He attempted to reveal man's concrete and personal attitude towards God and, on the other hand, to maintain the Cartesian antithesis between thought (soul) and extension (body). Malebranche did not, however, seek refuge in the Cartesian doctrine of innate ideas or concepts. Concepts were, for him, the fruit of an intellectual intuition of God's being. In God, we find the knowledge of our clear and distinct ideas. God, then, is not simply the guarantee of our knowledge, as in Descartes, but the direct source of our knowledge. We do not, however, know God as a clear and distinct idea, because he transcends our understanding.

Descartes was unable to explain the interaction between the soul and the body. Malebranche made some progress by simply denying it. The soul, he maintained, could not be the cause of a bodily movement and something perceived by the senses could not be the cause of an idea. What, in such cases, appears to be an effect of the soul on the body or of the body on the soul is in reality the effect of God alone. God is the cause of all these effects and of all effects as such, since true causality is a divine attribute. Finite things only provide the occasion for God's intervention, hence the term 'occasionalism'.

Malebranche was anticipated in this occasionalism by ARNOLD GEULINCX (1624–69), who was born in Antwerp. At Louvain, he became a firm advocate of Descartes's philosophy. Later, he was converted to Calvinism and became a professor at Leiden. Geulincx certainly increased the influence of

Descartes in the Netherlands and his interpretation of Descartes was probably of great importance to BENEDICTUS (BARUCH) DE SPINOZA (1632–77). Born in Amsterdam of Portuguese Jewish parents, Spinoza was quite early in his life expelled from the synagogue because of his progressive ideas. Because his life was threatened, he was obliged to leave Amsterdam and eventually he settled in the Hague. His upbringing had made him familiar with the many-sided and to a great extent neo-Platonic tradition of Jewish Arabic thought. He was also acquainted with the Platonism of the Renaissance and late scholasticism. Above all, however, he knew the work of Descartes. His own most important work, the *Ethica*, was published posthumously in the year of his death.

Controversy has for a long time raged over the fundamental meaning of Spinoza's work. Is it, as it would seem to be from the mathematically arranged *Ethica*, a rationalism carried through to its extreme limits, or is this rationalism rather at the service of an ultimate mystical vision? In my view, only the second interpretation can do full justice to Spinoza's thought. He was, in the last resort, concerned with the *amor intellectualis Dei*, the thinking love for God. His work was a continuously repeated effort to reach unity in love with God by thought. The system and structure of Spinoza's thought was essentially influenced by Descartes, but its real purport was quite different. In the case of Descartes, God was the ultimate guarantee of thought and thus, in a sense, outside thought itself. In the case of Spinoza, however, God was the ultimate goal of thought, aimed at from the very beginning in thought and even sustaining thought. Spinoza's idea of God was also quite different from Descartes's. For Descartes, God was a Person and the Creator of the world. For Spinoza, God was the all-embracing unity who expressed himself in the world.

For Spinoza, God was the independent 'substance'. By substance, he meant 'what is in itself and is understood from itself, that is to say, the concept of which does not need the concept of anything else by which it is formed'. This substance thus depends on nothing else and has its ground or basis in itself. It is its own cause, *cause sui*. Its existence is the necessary consequence of its essence and it can only be thought of as existing. Only one such substance is possible. If there were two such substances, there would be a mutual relationship and thus a certain dependence, which implies an inner contradiction. This one, independent substance is therefore infinite, because nothing conceivable can fall outside it—it is the absolutely infinite being, in other words, God.

If there can be nothing outside God, what is the world? The world is not identical with God, but the necessary expression of God. The world, as a unity of a multiplicity of modes of being (*modi*), is in God as an expression in multiplicity of the unity of his being. The relationship between God and the world is both logical and causal. It is logical because 'everything that is is in God and without God nothing can be or be understood.' It is causal because all finite existence is caused by God's existence. The logical bond, which is based on the affinity of being, indicates the unity of God and the world. The causal bond, which is based on the fact of existence, emphasizes the difference between God and the world. God is essentially activity and, as such, he is *natura naturans*, productive nature, as against the *natura naturata*, produced nature, of the world. Since this activity is the essence of God, he necessarily produces the world, but this necessity is not opposed to, but identical with freedom. Freedom is found in a being's acting from the necessity of its own nature and in its being determined by itself to act.

This twofold—logical and causal—bond, which unites God and the world, enables us to understand both the unity of finite beings and their difference. They are one in so far as they have their essence (*essentia*) *in* God and different in so far as they have their existence (*existentia*) *from* God. As a result of their difference, finite beings are limited by each other and dependent on each other. In their essence, they are eternal truth, whereas, in their existence, they are dependent on other finite beings, even though all existence ultimately comes from God.

God is in the world in two manners which we know as his attributes. These are thought and extension. Both these ways—the infinity of thought and the infinity of extension—lead us to a knowledge of God. This does not, however, mean that these are the only divine attributes. God has an infinite number of attributes, but we can only know those attributes that are revealed to us in the world. These attributes reveal themselves to us in the finite beings of the world, but, just as finite beings can only be understood as modes of being (*modi*) of God, who expresses himself in the world, so too can the attributes of God only be understood as essential qualities of God, which he communicates to finite beings in his realization of the world.

The more perfect a being is, the more real it is. Because of his power of thought, man is the most real among finite beings. In his essence, man is being-in-God. In his existence, he is a being-in-the-world. Since God is essentially activity, man is also in his essence activity. As existence, however, man is a subject of the worldly sphere. As essence, man is soul, that is, thought, since thought is not a faculty of the soul, but, as with Descartes, the soul itself. As existence, however, man is body, that is, extension, and therefore subject to the necessity of natural events. Man as such is never either pure activity or pure passivity. His activity is always mixed with passivity and his activity is never completely submerged in passivity. The more active man is (in thought), the more perfect and real he is, and the more subject he is to the passivity of the body, the more imperfect and unreal he is. Thinking activity is the beholding of everything in its universal idea as situated in God. In our passive corporeality, we are the victims of imagination, which shows us the individual as the real. Thus man is at first always in error and he can only set himself free from error by thought. If man succeeds in finding his own essence by thought, he will also find God, in whom his essence is contained, and he will see everything from the perspective of God in the light of eternity—*sub species aeternitatis*.

Man's will is not essentially different from his thinking, but is the activity of thought itself. In willing, man strives to realize his own essence as this is in God as an idea. Willing is self-realization, but, since this self-realization takes place by thinking, 'willing and thinking are one and the same'. The freedom of the will as a freedom of choice between two possibilities is denied here, but it is upheld as the realization of the necessity of our essence as situated in God. Feeling or emotion is also a form of thinking. Emotion (*affectus*) is always movement, inclination or desire (*cupiditas*). This movement may be affection, in which case it is joy (*laetitia*), as a growing self-realization. It may, on the other hand, be aversion, in which case it is sadness (*tristitia*), as an alienation from oneself.

These two tendencies are fundamental to man—thinking self-realization in God and the will to preserve oneself in the world. The latter, however, makes man a slave to the world and robs him of his ability to find himself in God. What is more, inclination is active in both these fundamental tendencies, since inclination is an aspect of thought, which, as reason (*ratio*), governs man's thinking realization of himself and, as imagination (*imaginatio*), governs his will to preserve himself in the world. This accounts for the fact that joy and sadness prevail in both tendencies. Joy, if it somehow succeeds in approaching its object, becomes love; and sadness, in the same way, becomes hatred. If love and hatred are directed towards the future, they show themselves as hope and fear. If they are certain of their expectation, they become certainty and despair.

When man's need to realize himself in thought is on a higher plane than his need to preserve himself in the world, then the principle that 'the urge to understand is the only basis of virtue' is fully in force. Evil puts existence in the world in the place of thinking self-realization, whereas good is all striving to achieve this self-realization, in other words, living consciously and reflectively. Spinoza said, 'By virtue and power I mean the same thing'. But power should not be understood here as the domination of the outside world, but as the ability to realize the idea that is situated in God. By power, man finds his own essence and this striving is virtue. In the last resort, good is what is in accordance with reason—rationality and morality are identical. Since rationality is a striving towards self-realization, it is possible to say that morality is being one-self. The moral man is himself—he expresses his divine essence in his worldly existence. His happiness is moreover to be found not in morality that is given to him afterwards as a reward, but in morality itself, because it is man's happiness to express his essence in his existence. Thus man strives, in his self-realization in thinking love, towards God—*amor intellectualis Dei*, the thinking love for God.

Whereas Descartes's themes were developed by Malebranche and Spinoza in a mystical direction, the English school took a completely different course. The English philosophers did not by-pass Descartes's thought, but always saw rationalism in an empirical framework, as defined by Bacon. THOMAS HOBBES (1588–1679) combined empiricism and rationalism in the first consistently materialist philosophy of the modern age. The following is a very brief summary of his main ideas.

Philosophy is the one universal science. It is our knowledge, acquired by sound reasoning, of phenomena from their known causes and, vice versa, of possible causes from known phenomena. It has all the facts of perception or observation as its object and the knowledge of causes as its aim. Its means are concepts, expressed in words, which represent things. The objects that we know in the form of states of consciousness are present in perceptions. It is only in the sciences which produce their own object that we have certain knowledge. Science produces these objects by means of the concepts of time, space, number and movement which are perceived in moving bodies. It is only the movement of the smallest parts which seems to be real in these objects. All qualitative phenomena are emotions of the subject. States of consciousness must similarly be regarded as movements. All beings are causally determined in accordance with the mathematical and mechanical laws of nature. Thus, the world is a causal whole, of which states of consciousness form a part. This, of course, means that freedom is excluded.

The science of politics is no more than state mechanics. The individual members of a state submit themselves by contract to the state in order to be protected against each other, because, in his need for self-preservation, man is essentially the enemy of his fellows—*homo homini lupus*, man is a wolf to man. Individuals, therefore, cannot accept as valid any laws against the state. The state is supreme and recognizes no law other than its own well-being. Galilean and Cartesian ideas are clearly discernible in the philosophy of Hobbes, as well as the state despotism of the Italian Renaissance.

JOHN LOCKE (1632–1704) continued the empirical tradition. His main work was *An Essay concerning Human Understanding* (1690). Locke set himself the task of investigating 'the origin, certainty and extent of human knowledge, together with the grounds and degrees of belief, opinion and assent'. He was not interested in metaphysical speculations about the nature of mind and matter, but in describing our way of knowing.

First and foremost, Locke laid down that neither innate principles nor innate ideas are known to the human mind. Experience is the only source of all our knowledge. To begin with, our intellect is *tabula rasa*, a blank tablet, an unwritten page. Our experience is of two kinds—inward and external. External experience—'sensation' or sensory perception—provides us with our idea of external objects. Inward experience—'reflection'—provides us with our idea of the activity of our mind upon the ideas gained by perception—inward perception, thought, doubt, belief, reasoning, knowing, willing and all the other activities of the mind. Ideas can be either 'simple' or 'complex'. Complex ideas can be traced back to simple ideas. Faced with these simple ideas, which are gained directly by external perception, our mind is absolutely passive. It combines these simple ideas to form complex ideas. By comparison, further ideas come into being. These are the 'ideas of relation'—our ideas of temporal, spatial and causal relationships, for example. Dissociation and abstraction lead to our 'general ideas'. The most important complex idea is that of 'substance'. Whenever several simple ideas occur regularly together, we regard them as belonging to one and the same thing, which we then call the substance. This, however, is only a term for something that we do not know.

It is only in judgement that we can speak of truth and falsehood. Judgement is simply the perception of 'agreement or disagreement' between two ideas. This agreement or disagreement can occur in four ways—firstly, identity or diversity, secondly, relation, thirdly, 'co-existence' or necessary connection and fourthly, real existence. However divergent these four ways of agreement or disagreement may be, there is in each of them a combination of ideas. They come therefore to the attention of the mind and the truth of our judgement is known in 'intuitive knowledge'. It is on this that we base all our certainty and evidence. Argument has less evidence than intuition because it has to have recourse to the memory. If it is to be valid, every element of deduction must possess intuitive evidence. Intuition and argument provide the certainty of knowledge. Apart from these, at least as far as general judgements are concerned, there are only 'belief' and 'opinion', since knowledge can merely avail itself of the direct data of sensory perception.

In his *Essay*, Locke also provided a proof of the existence of God. Taking his own existence as his starting-point, he argued that there must be a cause which has existed from all eternity and which is the principle and source of all beings and consequently omnipotent and omniscient. This cause Locke called God and he moreover regarded divine revelation as indisputably necessary, although it was, in his view, also necessary for man to be able to approve intellectually the content of revelation—it could not contain anything that was quite alien to the human intellect. The Christian revelation satisfied all these demands and, for Locke, Christianity was consequently the most reasonable of all religions. This raised the question of natural religion, which became a prominent theme in the eighteenth and nineteenth centuries.

PIERRE BAYLE (1647–1706), the son of a French Protestant minister who spent most of his life in the Netherlands, was even more averse from systematization than Locke. Bayle was a hypercritical thinker who had no firm convictions, but who employed his mercilessly critical mind in the search for weak spots. His *Dictionnaire historique et critique* (1695–7) was in every respect a revolutionary book. In accordance with his belief that the human intellect was very suitable for the work of tracing errors, but not suited to discovering the truth and to offering certainty, Bayle was never constructive. He had a very great influence on French philosophy of the eighteenth century, but before this time all the abundant ideas of the seventeenth century were brought together by Leibniz.

Germany began to claim a share in European philosophy with GOTTFRIED WILHELM VON LEIBNIZ (1646–1716), although Leibniz himself wrote his works in French. His work was a constant dialogue with Descartes, Malebranche, Geulincx, Spinoza, Locke and Bayle. More than any of these philosophers, however, Leibniz reverted again and again to scholastic ideas (his thorough knowledge of Aristotle was one reason for this). He never wrote a comprehensive work of philosophy, because his life was far too much taken up with practical activities, beginning with the founding of the Berlin *Sozietat der Wissenschaften* and ending with his attempts to reunite the churches. Many of his ideas were expressed in his correspondence and a great deal of his work is not even yet published, including much in the field of logic, in which he was a pioneer. He was indeed the forerunner of modern logistics. But in every sphere Leibniz was a universal spirit—in jurisprudence, philology, history, theology and, like all the great minds of the period, in mathematics and physics. He discovered differential and integral calculus at the same time as Newton. He attempted to overcome the antithesis between empiricism and rationalism. Although he never succeeded in systematizing his ideas, both his work and his life were dominated by an earnest desire for harmony.

Whereas, for Spinoza, there was only one independent unit or 'substance', God's all-embracing unity, Leibniz took as his point of departure man's experience of himself, through which the self comes to know itself as an independent being. This being is, as such, activity—thinking and willing. As a 'simple' or individual being (*ens singulare*), it is different from all other individual beings and its activity is, in the first place, an unfolding of itself. Thus the universe consists of individual beings (monads) which, as independent units, cannot exert any real influence on each other. There is, in the infinite number of these independent units, an essential gradation, since both lifeless and living beings—animals and men, pure spirits and God—are monads. In addition to being essentially independent and individual, the monad is also essentially active and, as an unfolding of itself, the monad's activity is, in the first place, consciousness. This consciousness is present in varying degrees —it is latent in lifeless things, primitive in plants, sensory in animals, intellectual in man, spiritual in pure spirits and un-limited and all-embracing in God. In man, however, various forms of consciousness are present at the same time, so that latent consciousness, for example, also plays an important part in his case.

If the monads cannot have an influence on each other, how is it possible to explain the order of the world? Leibniz explained this by calling the monads 'windowless'—although they are not influenced by other monads, each monad reflects in its own way, as a microcosm, the macrocosm or universe. If, then, there is an interaction between the monads, this can only be explained by a harmony, established by God from the beginning, between them (*harmonie préétablie*). The harmony of the monads works like that of clocks which were set in motion at the same time and which continue to run together. Anyone seeing these clocks might assume that they are made to function by some invisible shared mechanism, whereas their running together is in fact due only to the ingenuity of the clock-maker who previously brought about their harmony.

As the monads are constantly striving towards clearer consciousness, the universe is always developing towards a higher level of consciousness. This striving is present in every human being. Leibniz's philosophy certainly contained the idea of a kind of spiritualization of the body, in which he was unable to overcome Descartes's dualism. In man, body and soul only apparently work together by virtue of the *harmonia praestabilita*. There is no interaction between them. There is, however, a certain unity because the monad of the soul thinks the body and thus gives the monads of the body their specific unity (*vinculum substantiale*).

Two forms of truth are known to man. By his intellect he can discover the eternal truths, the *vérités de raison*, which are valid because they are in themselves absolutely necessary, and by experience he can discover the factual truths, the *vérités de fait*, which are inferred by induction from perception. They concern the intellect only in so far as they can be traced back to the eternal truths. Unlike Spinoza, Leibniz upheld the freedom of the will which, he claimed, was to be found in the intensity with which man himself collaborated in his spiritual unfolding of himself, his highest moral task.

Unlike Spinoza too, Leibniz insisted on the idea of a personal God and, to support his claim, he used not only the cosmological and teleological arguments of scholasticism but also the ontological argument of Anselm and Descartes in an amended form. That, in the essence of which existence is contained, must, if it has an essence, in other words, if it is (positively) possible, also really exist. Such a being is God, who exists if he is possible. But he is possible and therefore he exists. In his *Théodicée* (*Essais de théodicée sur la bonté de Dieu, la liberté de l'homme et l'origine du mal*, 1710), Leibniz dealt with the problem of evil in the world. Metaphysical evil is the necessary limitation of the finite, that is, of everything that is not God. Physical evil, pain, and moral evil, sin, are a consequence of this necessary metaphysical evil. God, however, ultimately directs this evil to the realization of good and it is towards this that man must also strive. Leibniz was of the opinion that many worlds were possible, but that God created the best world, in which evil was restricted to the most narrow limits but continued to be necessary so as to make man conscious of his finiteness and his freedom. With this optimism, Leibniz anticipated, more than any other of his contemporaries, the optimistic view of the world of the eighteenth century Enlightenment.

3. *The Enlightenment*

The period of the 'Enlightenment' was characterized by the general prevalence of a spirit of optimism and confidence in the intellectual power of European thought. A self-assured middle class began to take up an increasingly important place in scientific life. The optimism of the eighteenth century, however, was above all due to the extremely rapid development of mathematics and physics. An enormous influence was exerted by ISAAC NEWTON (1642–1727), who laid the foundations of modern physics and opened the way to an almost unlimited development of this study. Important results had been achieved in mathematics, biology, philology and history and eighteenth century thinkers were consequently confident that great progress would also be made in these fields. In the long run, more was expected from the positive sciences than from philosophy, with the result that the eighteenth century was not a period in which philosophy flourished. Any important achievements that were made were either in the sphere of criticism or on the borderline between philosophy and the positive sciences.

The most important figure of the German Enlightenment was CHRISTIAN WOLFF (1679–1754), who systematized the philosophy of Leibniz and emphasized especially its optimistic and rationalist aspects. He also demonstrated that both moral teaching and all natural teaching about God were entirely dependent on religion. His thought had a distinctly deistic tendency—God created the world, but then left it to follow its own course. Leibniz's philosophy, interpreted and deprived of its depth by Wolff, exerted an extremely powerful influence on German thought in the eighteenth century. Wolff was the first to use the German language consistently and his example was followed by the countless 'popular philosophers' as they were called who perpetuated the spirit of the Enlightenment. The most important work of these philosophers was in the sphere of aesthetics, which they examined for the first time in a systematic manner.

A pantheistic vision of God, man and the world was developed by GOTTHOLD EPHRAIM LESSING (1729–81), who provided a philosophy of history in his *Erziehung des Menschengeschlechtes* (1780). Lessing maintained that there was no reality apart from God and that the world was in God and originated by God's conceiving his perfections as different from himself, so that the development of the world was simply the progressive thinking of God. Mankind was included in this development and was always moving towards a higher state of perfection. Judaism and Christianity were, in Lessing's view, simply stages in this development. Religion could not be independent of historical facts and the goal of this historical development was a pure natural religion.

There was little that was revolutionary in German philosophy of the eighteenth century. English philosophy, however, developed rapidly, from Locke via Berkeley to Hume, in the direction of empirical scepticism. GEORGE BERKELEY (1685–1753) took perception as his starting-point for human knowledge—there are no general ideas, but only concrete perceptions and all our knowledge is based on these. A perception does not, however, imply that there is something outside our perception of which we can obtain knowledge in perception. There is nothing other than 'being perceived' itself—being is being perceived (*esse est percipi*). Concepts like substance, matter, world and so on are therefore without meaning. It is, however, possible to enquire about the self, for whom all perceptions are present. This self is a perceiving, active spirit, a 'spiritual substance' and the cause of my perceptions. But this causal being is only fully applicable to my memory and my imagination and not to my original perceptions which, because of their powers, are distinct from all the images of my memory. My spirit is certainly the cause of my *being able* to have these perceptions, but God is the cause of my in fact having them. God gives us the spectacle of a material world, but this does not in any way exist in itself. Man is not alone, because God does not give this spectacle to him alone, but to all men. In the last resort, this spectacle has its intransient existence in the eternal consciousness of God.

In Berkeley's thought, God had, so to speak, to come to the rescue of reality and Berkeley thus forsook the purely descriptive point of view that he inherited from Locke. Non-empirical concepts such as substance and cause continued to play an important part in the philosophy of both Berkeley and Locke. DAVID HUME (1711–76) aimed to carry out Locke's programme consistently, in other words, to give a description of human knowledge without recourse to non-empirical factors. His *Treatise of Human Nature*, which he later condensed and published as *An Enquiry concerning Human Understanding*, was written in this spirit.

In consciousness, a distinction must be made between 'impressions' and 'ideas'. Impressions come about as a result of outward or inward perception—they are clear and vivid. Concepts or ideas are, as it were, derivations, and they contain nothing more than is contained in the original impressions. The factors that are similar in a number of different impressions are brought together and vaguely summarized in our concepts. As there are only 'impressions' and 'ideas' in our consciousness, there is little reason for us to call the self a substance like the things of the outside world. I am simply the continuous stream of sensations and experiences that constitutes my consciousness. I am this stream, not what sustains it—I am completely merged into this stream. The concept substance has as little meaning as the concept being. We never perceive anything other than that two phenomena regularly succeed each other. In such cases, we speak of cause and effect, but the influence exerted by the first phenomenon on the second is not entirely contained in the succession. The concepts substance and cause are based on 'belief' and they are not met with in our sensations. In this way, Hume pursued Locke's teaching to the point where it became complete scepticism.

In his later writings, Hume reduced ethics to social feelings and rejected all revealed religion. A natural religion cannot rely on rational arguments, but it can often be of practical use. Hume's ultimate working out of Locke's principles of human knowledge thus led to a result that was very different from the one which the Christian, Berkeley, who strove to base the necessity of revelation on the very weakness of the human capacity for knowing, would have expected or desired.

Locke, Berkeley and Hume were mainly concerned with the theory of knowing. Hobbes, Shaftesbury and Reid, on the other hand, were principally interested in ethics. A clear line of development runs from Locke via Berkeley to Hume. No such line is discernible in English ethics from Hobbes to Shaftesbury and Reid. Both Shaftesbury and Reid developed their ethics in open conflict with Hobbes and, what is more, their ideas were mutually very different. Although there have been repeated attempts in English ethics to see ethics separately from a more comprehensive system of philosophical thought, as with Hobbes, this does not occur in the case of Shaftesbury and Reid.

ANTHONY SHAFTESBURY (1671–1713) took an analysis of moral activity as his point of departure. A special form of judgement is implied in moral activity. This judgement, however, is not the same as intellectual judgement, but is more in accordance with the method of working of feeling. In this context, Shaftesbury used the term 'moral sense' or 'taste'. This moral sense is a certain inclination which declares itself in favour of or against a certain action. It would, however, be wrong to equate the moral sense with feeling. In its manner of functioning, it is to some extent analogous to feeling, but in itself it is as distinct from feeling as the intellect is. It is very similar to the sense of beauty. Both the good and the beautiful are recognized in a spontaneous judgement, but morality is not completely absorbed in this spontaneous judgement. This judgement is inwardly perceived by us and thus gives rise to speculation about ourself. This speculation about ourself on the one hand and the practical exercise of our moral judgement on the other together give rise to true morality, which enables us to order our life harmoniously. If our life is thus ordered, it is in accordance with our nature, which itself forms a part of the universal harmony of the cosmos in which everything that exists has a share.

The thought of THOMAS REID (1710–96), the leader of the Scottish school, took a different course. He maintained that man had a number of innate 'original and natural' judgements in the spheres of knowledge and of action, which were the first principles which guide us in our first acts of thought and our first actions (the 'principles of common sense'). These principles are quite evident to the common sense of every man and the philosopher should therefore not overthrow them, but try to locate them, clarify them and establish them by argument. As examples of these principles of common sense, Reid cited the principle of the necessary attribution of qualities to a substance, that of cause and effect, that of the identity of the individual self, that of the existence of the outside world, that of freedom and that of responsibility. It was, in his opinion, only in this way that it was possible to uphold the reality of our power to know and of true morality.

The ideas of Locke and Shaftesbury on the one hand and the optimism of Leibniz on the other formed the point of departure for the Enlightenment in France. The great systems of the seventeenth century were regarded with increasing suspicion and the aim of the eighteenth-century French thinkers was to achieve a critical, analytical philosophy in the spirit of Locke.

CHARLES DE MONTESQUIEU (1689-1755) carried on the tradition of jurisprudence of the preceding centuries and his theory of the *trias politica*, that is, the division of the three powers into the legislative, the executive and the judicial power, in his most important work, *De l'esprit des lois* (1748), had an enormous influence on the subsequent history of politics.

VOLTAIRE (François Marie Arouet, 1694-1778) also had a very great influence on later thought. He was a decided eclectic, but he knew how to choose the things that appealed to his contemporaries and to express them in a brilliant way. Locke, Shaftesbury and Newton strongly influenced him, but he also followed with great pliancy the later developments of the French Enlightenment. He was above all a rationalist and, although he was convinced of the existence of God as the Creator of the world, as a deist he was strongly opposed to any form of revealed religion, believing that God, after creation, simply left the world to its fate.

ETIENNE DE CONDILLAC (1715-80) was a much more original philosopher, who took an analysis of Locke as his starting-point and from this developed a considerable body of ideas. His most important work was his *Traité des sensations* (1754). Experience was, for Condillac, the beginning and the end of all knowledge, and Condillac made no distinction between inward and external experience. As far as conscious thought is concerned, everything is 'sensation' which comes about by the mechanical effect of the outside world. Various sensations combine to form the more complex conscious ideas. 'Attention' is a very powerful sensation and, if this persists in the presence of a new sensation, we then speak of 'memory'. A comparison between two sensations gives rise to 'judgement', a repetition of which causes 'reflection'. 'Imagination' prevails whenever a previous sensation proves superior in strength to a present sensation. Since all sensations are, of necessity, either pleasant or unpleasant, all forms of willing (*vouloir*) and desire (*désir*) arise from these sensations. Finally, our general ideas of number, possibility, duration, succession and so on come about when we consider what these sensations have in common. Despite his consistently worked out sensualism, Condillac was not a materialist, because he was convinced that the singularity of our perception pointed to something that was essentially different from the extension of matter. Condillac's influence on French philosophy of his own time was very great. It resulted in many cases in complete materialism. On the other hand, however, a spiritualistic tradition, which drew its inspiration from many other sources and culminated in the work of Maine de Biran, persisted in France. Condillac's ideas about the building up of the sciences on the basis of a system of concepts controlled by experience anticipated the work of Comte.

Several of Condillac's contemporaries developed a completely materialist philosophy. The most consistent and sound materialist system of thought at this time was formulated by PAUL D'HOLBACH, for whom only matter and movement had real existence, the rest being illusion. Everything that happened in the world came about, according to d'Holbach, because of a mechanical necessity, of which man, as a part of nature, was only a part—his consciousness was an aspect of matter. There could, of course, be no place in a system of this kind for God (unless nature were made absolute and thus became God), immortality, free will and morality.

The influence of the eighteenth-century French materialists and of d'Holbach especially, great though it was, was surpassed by that of the encyclopaedists. The first two volumes of the famous *Encyclopédie* appeared in 1751 and, after having been banned again and again, the last volumes were published in 1766. Under the inspiring leadership of Diderot and d'Alembert, the *Encyclopédie* became a mainstay of the ideas of the Enlightenment and, in addition to the work of Voltaire, it was the most important instrument in spreading these ideas.

Although he shared neither the optimism nor the rationalism of the enlightened philosophers, JEAN-JACQUES ROUSSEAU (1712–78) is usually included among them. Rousseau was an optimist in that he regarded man as essentially good. Man was, in Rousseau's view, unspoilt in his natural state, but lost his innocence and became corrupt with the advance of civilization. Man's task, then, was to return to nature. Rousseau's optimism about man's essential nature was thus accompanied by a deep pessimism about his real condition and, unlike the rationalist philosophers of the Enlightenment, he did not expect this condition to be improved by the progress of science, but rather to be made worse. In his opinion, therefore, man's intellect could not act as a guide to human conduct, because its reasoning was misleading. Only feeling could provide this guidance, because, in feeling, man was directly addressed by the pure voice of nature.

Civilization has caused society to become degenerate. Morality, which is based on feeling, has become an intellectual set of rules, reason has led to the development of a materialistic science in which man has no place and natural human emotions have been distorted into conventions and regulations. Civilization begins when man begins to produce more than he needs and consequently begins to stimulate his natural needs artificially. The resulting surplus is shared unequally and provides the basis for the difference between rich and poor and those with power and those without power. All wealth and power is usurpation and a consequence of the unleashing of evil passions.

Rousseau believed that there were two principal ways of improving man's condition—on the one hand, it could be improved by a natural education of the individual (*Émile*) and, on the other, by a better organization of the state (*Le contrat social*). In the latter work, he argued that, since the state came about as the result of a voluntary agreement between individuals, every member of the state ought to have equal rights and to be a free citizen, and that sovereign power should be in the hands of all the people. In affairs of state, the general will (*volonté générale*) should be decisive. This general will is not, however, the same as the will of everyone (*volonté de tous*). Rousseau was not able to explain, however, how the general will ought to be expressed, because, in his view, it no more coincided with the will of the majority than it did with the will of everyone.

4. The Critique of Knowledge

IMMANUEL KANT (1724–1804) was also an eighteenth-century philosopher in whose work the Enlightenment reached, so to speak, an unexpected flowering and who at the same time pointed to the future of philosophy. In his own opinion, he was an 'enlightened' thinker and this is also clear from his ideas about society. Although he was, in a certain sense, in the tradition of the encyclopaedists, his true philosophical inspiration arose from a clash between the German metaphysical thought of Wolff's school and the English empirical thought of Hume. This led him to the decisive question as to which elements in human thought derived from experience and which were inherent in our thought as such.

Kant spent his whole life at Königsberg, where he became a professor in 1770. His early works, written before 1770, were not fundamentally different from the prevailing philosophical views. After a period of silence, however, he published his *Kritik der reinen Vernunft* (*Critique of Pure Reason*) in 1781, a second, and considerably amended edition of which appeared in 1787. His two other fundamentally important works were his *Kritik der praktischen Vernunft* (*Critique of*

Practical Reason, 1788) and his *Kritik der Urteilskraft* (*Critique of Judgement,* 1790).

There is, in the work of Kant's second period, a gradual development. This, however, presents us with so many problems that we cannot deal with it here and must limit ourselves to Kant's basic ideas as revealed in these three works. In this, we shall again have to confine ourselves to an examination of two main spheres of Kantian thought—his theory of knowledge and his ethics. It will, however, be seen that these two spheres are not entirely dissociated from each other, but that they supplement each other in a single synthesis. We shall be able only to touch in passing on various other Kantian themes.

To begin with, however, we shall mention briefly the influences which made themselves felt in Kant's thought. It is clear from his earliest writings that he originally accepted the metaphysics of the rationalists. According to his own confession, however, Hume roused him from his dogmatic slumber and the period of silence which preceded the publication of the *Critique* was a period during which he was struggling to find a new way out of the clash between rationalist metaphysics and empirical scepticism. A great deal of this is clear from the inaugural speech which Kant gave when he became ordinary professor at Königsberg in 1770. But his ideas were not fully mature until 1781.

In his critique of knowledge, Kant's object was to define the value and the extent of all human knowledge. He was convinced that thought had found its permanent direction in natural science, as established by Newton. What, then, can we learn, Kant asked, about knowing as such from a critical examination of natural scientific knowing? In the first place, critical speculation about knowing will teach us something about the value and extent of knowledge and thus about the conditions for thought that can be scientifically metaphysical.

This critical speculation about knowledge is contained in the *Critique of Pure Reason*. Moreover, since knowledge is based on judgement, an investigation into the nature of judgement is also necessary.

Judgement is a combination of two concepts—subject and predicate. This combination can be either analytic or synthetic, that is to say, the predicate may be already contained in the subject, in which case the judgement is analytic, or the predicate may add something new to the concept of the subject, in which case the judgement is synthetic. The judgement, all bodies are extended, is analytic, because extension is inherent in the body as such. An analytic judgement simply clarifies the conceptual content of the subject. The judgement, some bodies are heavy, is synthetic, because the predicate does not apply to the body as such, but only to some bodies. The synthetic judgement thus provides new knowledge.

The combination of which judgement consists may also be *a posteriori* or *a priori*. A judgement the origin of which is to be found in experience is *a posteriori*. Every judgement the only origin of which is to be found in reason is *a priori*. It would therefore appear that all *a posteriori* judgements are synthetic judgements, because only experience can lead to synthesis, in other words, a new insight. It would also seem to be obvious that all *a priori* judgements are analytic judgements, because reason only leads to a further analysis of what is already given. This obvious conclusion, however, is false. There are also synthetic *a priori* judgements. It is from this kind of judgement that mathematics is constructed and with which scientifically justified metaphysics has to operate.

Science presupposes judgements which provide new knowledge, in other words, synthetic judgements. It also presupposes judgements which are necessary and universal, in other words, *a priori* judgements. *A posteriori* judgements are, after all, dependent on constantly changing experience and cannot therefore be necessary or universal. Science therefore demands synthetic *a priori* judgements. There are certain truths in which reason establishes a necessarily and universally valid bond between subject and predicate, although the predicate is not contained in the subject. These are precisely those truths which are fundamental to science. But how are they possible? The judgement, everything that happens has its cause, is necessarily and universally valid, but at the same time it is also synthetic, because the concept cause is not contained in the concept happen. What, then, is the *a priori* connection between these two concepts, which are not contained in each other?

It is possible to say that Kant wrote his *Critique of Pure Reason* to provide an answer to this question. Even in his introduction to the work, Kant made a distinction between pure *a priori* knowledge and experiential *a posteriori* knowledge. Pure *a priori* knowledge comes only from reason. It is peculiar to reason and is therefore active even in everyday thought. Philosophy, however, needs a science which will define the possibility, the principles and the scope of *a priori* knowledge. It is therefore necessary to bear in mind the difference between analytic and synthetic judgements and to remember that synthetic *a priori* judgements are contained as principles in all the theoretical sciences. If these judgements are shown to be at the root of all mathematics and natural science, it should be possible to go on to trace their significance for metaphysics.

Up till now, metaphysics has not been able to establish itself on a firm scientific basis and, as a result, the study has lost its prestige. It is, however, a natural human aptitude to practise metaphysics and the philosopher must therefore try to find the principles according to which metaphysics can develop as a real science. To do this, it may be necessary to cut down the entire growth of the centuries and to go back to the very root of metaphysics to allow a new plant to grow again. In so doing, however, it should not be forgotten that two shoots of human knowledge may grow from the same unknown root—the senses and the intellect. Objects are given to us by our senses and are thought by the intellect.

Kant was emphatic in maintaining that his *Critique* was not written in order to provide a system of transcendental philosophy, but simply in order to provide the opportunity for such a system to be developed. Kant called transcendental the knowledge which is not concerned with objects as such, but with our way of knowing objects, in so far as this knowledge is *a priori* possible. His *Critique* was therefore constructed in the following way. In the first place, it was divided into the *Transzendentale Elementarlehre* and the *Transzendentale Methodenlehre*. In the *Transzendentale Elementarlehre*, Kant examined critically the *a priori* elements in our knowledge. In accordance with the distinction that he made between sensory perception and intellect, he subdivided the *Elementarlehre* into *Die transzendentale Ästhetik* and *Dietranszendentale Logik*.

The 'Transcendental Aesthetics'—Kant used the word aesthetics in its original sense as relating to perception by the senses—deals with the conditions under which objects (*Gegenstände*) are given to us. Sensory perception includes two *a priori* forms—space and time. Space and time are *a priori* forms of our knowledge. Things themselves are not spatial and temporal, but our senses perceive them in the forms of space and time. What Kant himself called the Copernican revolution of his thought thus emerges very clearly here—our knowledge does not direct itself towards things, but things direct themselves towards our knowledge. Knowing is therefore not a passive representation of things, but an active formation of ideas. The content (or matter) of our knowledge certainly comes from things, but the form comes from knowledge itself. This at the same time results in our knowing not things as such (*das Ding an sich*), but only their appearance (*die Erscheinung*). Kant warned us emphatically not to identify appearance and semblance (*Schein*). Semblance does not relate in any way to reality. Appearance, on the other hand, is our way of knowing the reality of things.

By far the biggest part of Kant's *Critique* is the second part of the *Elementarlehre*, the 'Transcendental Logic', which deals with the *a priori* elements in intellectual knowledge. This section is again divided into *Die transzendentale Analytik* and *Die transzendentale Dialektik*. The 'Analytics' deals first with *a priori* concepts and then with *a priori* judgements. Kant gave the name categories to *a priori* concepts. Kant distinguished twelve categories and grouped them under four headings, each containing three categories, the third forming the connection between the first two. The first group, quantity, consists of the categories of unity, plurality and totality. The second, quality, consists of the categories of reality, negation and limitation. The third, relation, is shown in the categories of substance and accident, causality and community and the fourth group, modality, contains the categories of possibility, existence and necessity.

Sense-perception (*die Anschauung*) provides us with a disordered multiplicity of appearances or impressions (*Erscheinungen*). By means of the categories, the intellect achieves order in this multiplicity. The categories are the various forms in which the transcendental self thinks. The transcendental self is the self in so far as it is the condition for the unity of knowledge and is itself unconditional. Every act of thinking is of necessity accompanied by the thought, I think. This is the basis for the unity of knowledge (*Apperception*) which is the nodal point in which all forms of knowledge come together. Thus apperception, by means of the categories, reduces the disordered multiplicity of impressions to an ordered entirety of concepts. Here, too, it is evident that things have to direct themselves towards our knowledge and not vice versa.

How, then, are the categories applied to these appearances? This is done by our power of judgement (*Urteilskraft*), which bridges the gap between the appearances perceived by our senses and our intellectual concepts. Kant then goes on to describe the fundamental principles (*Grundsätze*) by which these appearances can be included among the categories. There are four main principles, one for each of the four groups of categories—the axioms of intuition for the categories of quantity, the anticipations of experience for those of quality, the analogies of experience for those of relation and the postulates of empirical thought in general for those of modality. These fundamental principles together comprise the system of synthetic *a priori* judgements and, on the basis of these principles, natural science is possible.

The 'Transcendental Analytics' thus performs the positive task of analyzing the intellectual elements in our knowledge into *a priori* concepts (categories) and *a priori* judgements (*Grundsätze*). The 'Transcendental Dialectics' performs the negative task of exposing transcendental semblance (*Schein*). Kant used the word dialectics in the sense of the medieval dialectica, which formed a part of logic and dealt with false conclusions. Whereas his 'Analytics' was concerned with an investigation of intellect and judgement, the 'Dialectics' consists of an examination of reason (*Vernunft*). Reason is the power to know principles (*Prinzipien*). The principle is a form of knowing which includes the particular among the general. We can continue reasoning until we are confronted with ultimate, irreducible principles. We are then confronted with the unconditional as such.

This unconditional is the idea. It appears in our thinking as the three ideas that govern all thought as the ideal—the ideas of the soul, of the world and of God. These ideas are not derived from experience. They are only regulative principles for experience, in contrast to the constitutive principles of the intellect which make experience as such possible. Because they are only regulative principles, it is fundamentally incorrect to regard these ideas as the ideas of existing realities (*Dinge an sich*). The soul, the world and God do not exist as things, but as the rules or postulates of our reason. Our reason cannot help thinking these ideas, but to regard these ideas as the ideas of existing things is the basic fault of traditional metaphysics.

Having made this clear in the introduction to and the first book of the 'Dialectics', the second book—by far the longest section of the 'Dialectics'—is devoted to a refutation of the traditional metaphysical proofs of the existence of the soul, the world and God. In its proofs of the existence of the soul, traditional metaphysics is guilty of false reasoning (paralogisms), because the concept of the soul always appears in a double sense (as a form of thinking and as a substance), with the result that the reasoning includes four instead of three terms and is therefore invalid (*quaternio terminorum*). In connection with the traditional cosmology, Kant spoke of antinomies. In every main group of categories, there is an inner antithesis, because, in respect of quantity, quality, relation and modality, two mutually contradictory theses can, with equal justice, be proved. Finally, Kant criticized the three great proofs of the existence of God—the ontological proof, the cosmological proof and the physico-theological proof from the existence of purposiveness. The ontological proof is an unjustified transference from the order of thought to that of existence and the other two proofs can also, in the last resort, be traced back to the ontological proof. The cosmological proof is based on the principle of causality, which does not lead us to transcend the world of phenomena. The physico-theological proof extends the idea of purposiveness beyond the scope of human knowledge, which is limited to experience. The real significance of the ideas is that they provide thought with a permanent direction and thus make the activity of thinking possible. It is therefore not a question of freeing oneself of these ideas, which is in any case impossible, but of understanding that they are purely regulative and are not ideas of existing things.

The *Transzendentale Methodenlehre* indicates, in a few short chapters, how a new metaphysics can be constructed after the purification suggested in the 'Dialectics' has taken place. Some of the ideas in the *Methodenlehre* anticipate the views expressed in Kant's later works, but it would appear that he intended to work them out fully in a last work that was never written. All that we have of this final work is a few preliminary studies.

Kant set out his moral teaching in his *Critique of Practical Reason*. In his *Critique of Pure Reason*, he attempted to throw light on the universal and necessary conditions for human knowledge. In the second of his great works, he dealt with the universal and necessary conditions for moral activity, examining what holds good for acting man as such and therefore for all men. At the very outset, a very important distinction is made between the conditions for action and those for knowing. Man is necessarily subject to the conditions for knowledge. With regard to the conditions for action, on the other hand, there is latitude for freedom. According to the rules indicated in the critique of knowledge, man must (*muß*), by virtue of natural necessity, think. According to the rules defined in the practical critique, man ought to (*soll*) act. Kant's moral doctrine is a formal ethical treatise—it does not set out the actions that concrete man ought to perform, but the principles that he should follow if he wishes to act morally.

Just as Kant made a distinction in his critique of knowledge between the form of thought that is inherent in thought itself and the content of thought that comes from the senses (*Anschauung*), so too did he distinguish in action between the form of our action, in other words, reasonable legality, and its content, that is, all the sensual inclinations that are inherent in man. Man's sensual inclinations are in the order of natural necessity. Reasonable legality, on the other hand, is in the order of freedom. Reasonable legality is revealed to the consciousness in the form of command. It is not a question of what reason commands, but of reason's commanding as such. Kant called this the autonomy of pure practical reason and regarded it as the only principle of morality. It is diametrically opposed to the heteronomy of the inclinations, which alienate reason from themselves.

This command can be revealed to the consciousness both subjectively and objectively in various ways. The maxim is the subjective guide to the individual's action. The imperative is the objective rational principle that compels the will to act and is universally and necessarily valid. It can, however, be either conditional (hypothetical) or unconditional (categorical). The conditional imperative is the action prescribed by the reason when I wish to reach a definite goal—for example, if I want to live, I must work. The imperative is unconditional, however, if it applies to everyone and in all circumstances simply and solely by virtue of the fact that we are human. The categorical imperative has no definite content—it is simply a formal 'ought' (*sollen*). It does not tell us *what* we ought to want, but *how* we ought to want.

Kant put forward the following definitive formulation of the categorical imperative—act in such a way that the maxim of your will can at the same time always be valid as the principle of a general law. Whenever man is in doubt, he must always ask himself what would happen to mankind if everyone acted according to this maxim. But, if the inclinations are always in conflict with the reasonable legality of the categorical imperative, what causes man to uphold the categorical imperative rather than follow his inclinations? He does this because of his sense of duty—'thou shalt' (*du sollst*). Anything that he does as a result of his inclinations can never be moral.

Only what he does from a sense of duty can be moral. Kant called this sense of duty 'reverence' (*Achtung*). An action is not really moral only if it is the result of duty—in that case it is only legal. It is moral only if it is done as the result of a feeling of reverence for duty. Reverence is the real motivating force in moral action.

Reverence for the moral law may be more precisely defined as reverence for human dignity. The moral law is, after all, in the order of freedom and it is only by following the moral law that we can respect the autonomy of the human personality. All that exists can be a means for us, but man, in his autonomy, is an end in himself. This means that I may never use another person purely as a means. Morality demands that I should revere human dignity in myself and in the other person, in other words, in all others. Kant thus gave his formal ethics a first content. It should also be pointed out how firmly opposed Kant was, in his ethical doctrine, to any attempt to make the furtherance of human happiness the principle of morality.

Finally, Kant argued that certain fundamental presuppositions, which he called the postulates of practical reason, were included in the fact of moral consciousness. Freedom, immortality and the existence of God were, in Kant's opinion, such postulates. We have already seen that, for Kant, freedom was presupposed by the entire moral consciousness, to such an extent that there could be no question of morality without freedom. Kant, however, maintained that freedom itself could not be proved in the theoretical sense—it could only be postulated as the necessary basis of morality (*du kannst, denn du sollst*—'you can because you ought to'). The same holds good for the other postulates. Immortality of the soul is the necessary culmination of ethical action, which would otherwise be meaninglessly broken off. In the infinite distance of immortality, duty and happiness, which are opposed to each other in earthly life, ultimately coincide. Immortality, how-ever, can be guaranteed only by the real existence of a personal God.

In Kant's first two great *Critiques*, the antithesis between the senses and the intellect was central. In the third *Critique*, he attempted to reconcile the senses and the intellect and to see them in a certain unity. In the first *Critique*, Kant con-sidered nature, in the second, freedom. In the *Critique of Judgement*, he tried to consider freedom in nature. To this end, he formulated the principle of purposiveness as the unity of nature and freedom. Purposiveness can be both subjective and objective. It is subjective when man relates the object directly to himself. This occurs in his experience of beauty and Kant analyzed this in the first part of his third great work, the *Kritik der ästhetischen Urteilskraft*, the 'Critique of Aesthetic Judgement.' Purposiveness is objective in the mutual relation-ship of objects towards each other. Kant discussed the way in which we know this objective purposiveness in the second part of his book, the *Kritik der teleologischen Urteilskraft*, the 'Critique of Teleological Judgement'.

The idea of beauty reveals itself to us in the form of a work of art. In a work of art, man recognizes an external or aesthetic purposiveness in that his pleasure conforms with the idea. Al-though this pleasure is subjective, it is not arbitrary, because a generally valid *a priori* is at work here in our imagination (*Einbildungskraft*). This pleasure, moreover, is not self-interested as is the case with sensual inclinations, but disinterested. The idea of purposiveness shows itself as objectively realized in the things of nature. Because of this teleological *a priori*, we can see this inner purposiveness in natural phenomena by intuitive understanding. This purposiveness of nature lies in nature's orientation towards a logical system that is an accordance with our powers of comprehension.

This, then, is Kant's thought in its broadest outlines. His

great achievement was to subject the whole field of traditional philosophy to searching criticism and to open up perspectives to subsequent philosophers, even though he did not himself make a positive extension to philosophy. His influence has been exceptionally great and is still great even today. He made an especially deep impression on German thought. His criticism soon disposed of the rationalist metaphysics in the tradition of Wolff.

This was, however, not the case with another philosophical trend which was not, as Kant was, primarily concerned with how knowledge functions in natural science, but was directed towards the reality of history. To the philosophers of this school, man seemed to be involved in the historical reality with all his being, will and feeling. This school of thought was strongly represented in German philosophy of the eighteenth and nineteenth centuries and it persisted alongside the Kantian tradition, emerging powerfully, for example, in the work of Schelling and Hegel. Among the leading figures in this movement were JOHANN GEORG HAMANN (1730-88), FRIEDRICH HEINRICH JACOBI (1743-1819) and JACOB FRIEDRICH FRIES (1773-1843). A very important thinker in the sphere of language and history was JOHANN GOTTFRIED HERDER (1744-1803).

4 The Nineteenth Century

In the period of the Enlightenment, philosophical ideas became widely disseminated, but only Kant reached a pinnacle in human thought. The first half of the nineteenth century was an especially rich period of philosophical renewal. Great thinkers opened up entirely new fields of thought and asked questions which even today are still of the greatest importance. The formation of national traditions in philosophy which began in the preceding centuries led in the nineteenth to a German, a French and an English tradition. These three great national traditions in philosophy, which, although they certainly had contact with each other, preserved their own individual mode of thought, formed the basic framework of nineteenth-century philosophy.

1. *German Philosophy*

It was, of course, Kant who gave the German philosophical tradition of the nineteenth century its special character. The great thinkers who emerged in Germany during the first half of the century—Fichte, Schelling, Hegel and the others—regarded themselves as accomplishing the task set by Kant. But this is only to a certain extent true. Kant himself considered his most important task as a philosopher to be the careful definition of the frontiers of human knowledge and this and the precise Kantian distinction between knowledge of what is perceptible and human thought about what is not perceptible are lacking in the German philosophers who followed him. These thinkers returned to metaphysics, but their metaphysics do not fulfil the criteria laid down by Kant. Despite the undeniable greatness of these philosophers and despite the emergence later of a neo-Kantian school, essential tasks set by Kant were never in fact accomplished. This does not in any way diminish the greatness of the trio, Fichte, Schelling and Hegel. They developed so many new and fruitful ideas and methods that they are rightly regarded as very great philosophers indeed. Although they did not follow his thought in all its essential elements, they were certainly inspired by Kant.

JOHANN GOTTLIEB FICHTE (1762-1814) was the first to make a definitive step forward after Kant. His whole philosophy was embraced by the term that he himself used in many of his writings—*Wissenschaftslehre,* or the doctrine of knowledge.

What is this doctrine of knowledge? It is not a theoretical speculation about the structure of the separate sciences or spheres of knowledge and the connection between them, but a speculation about knowing itself. What is the basic condition that makes knowing as such possible? Before developing his own ideas in the light of this question, Fichte stipulated that there were two possible standpoints in philosophy—dogmatism (in the spirit of Wolff) and criticism (in the spirit of Kant)—and the choice made would depend on what sort of person the philosopher was. The two possibilities were unable to refute each other, because the choice was, for Fichte, a primary fact—dogmatism aimed to explain consciousness from things, whereas criticism sought to explain things from consciousness. It will be clear from this preliminary observation, then, that will played an important part in Fichte's thought.

In his doctrine of knowledge, Fichte aimed to overcome the Kantian antithesis between pure and practical reason. The concept of the self, or ego, was central in Fichte's thought, and the unity of thought and freedom was, in his view, contained in this ego. Fichte developed the status of this non-empirical, but transcendental ego in three theses. The first thesis was 'the ego posits itself and *is* only by virtue of this positing of itself'. This positing is 'act' (*Tathandlung*). This thesis was amplified by Fichte by the complimentary antithesis, 'the ego posits a non-ego against itself'.

The ego posits itself in freedom as thought. By virtue of this free thought, the ego is absolute. In this positing of itself which takes place by thinking, the ego, as an independent unit, does not precede thought, but is itself this thinking. In the thesis in which the ego posits itself in thinking freedom, the ego would remain a captive within itself in undifferentiated unity if it did not posit the non-ego in the antithesis. This non-ego is, however, not something that is outside the ego, but the ego to be thought which posits itself against the thinking ego. It was only by this rupture within the unity of the ego that Fichte was able to include the world in his system.

So as not to allow the unity of the ego to be lost because of this inner rupture, Fichte added a necessary third thesis, the synthesis: 'the ego posits in the ego against the divisible ego a divisible non-ego'. 'Divisible' (*teilbar*) here means divided here and now in real unity. The ego and the non-ego must of necessity limit each other. If the ego were unlimited, then the non-ego would not be and if the non-ego were unlimited, then the ego would not be. But the non-ego is posited within the ego and the antithesis between the ego and the non-ego is within the ego as such. This is only possible by limitation. Fichte defined this limitation as the partial cancelling out of the reality of something by denial. Thus the denial of the antithesis partially cancels out the reality of the thesis in the limitation of the synthesis. This therefore brings us to the following two theses, firstly, 'the ego posits itself as determined by the non-ego' and secondly, 'the ego posits the non-ego as determined by the ego'. The first of these two theses forms the basis for theoretical thought, the second the basis for practical thought.

Theoretical thought teaches us how the ego constructs its own world, but can only gradually recognize itself as the builder of its own world. In perception (*Empfindung*), the world is completely opposed to and distinct from the ego, but if the ego is elevated by sensory reflection (*Anschauung*) to conception, this marks the beginning of the integration of the world and the ego. This reflection (*Anschauung*) is in turn spiritualized, first becoming intellect (*Verstand*), then judgement (*Urteilskraft*) and finally reason (*Vernunft*), at which stage the world is entirely merged into the ego and the ego becomes the identity of thinking and thought. Reason, however, always continues to be the realm of ideas, in other words, it is posited as the idea, but is never completely realized. This explains the connection between theoretical and practical reason and, at the same time, the primacy of the second. The ultimate absolute is, however, the duty to realize oneself completely.

Practical reason posits the non-ego as determined by the ego. The ego gains control of the non-ego here, by taking increasing possession of itself. It first overcomes the natural passions and rises to seek happiness. This is in turn overcome by a striving towards the good, which is finally transcended by true morality, man's pure sense of duty. Duty is the complete realization of freedom and this freedom is attained when the ego has embodied the non-ego completely in itself. But even here perfect freedom is an idea that is not given as a gift, but set as a task, and can only be approached more and more closely.

This perfect realization of the freedom of the ego does not, however, mean that others are of no importance to the ego.

On the contrary, the ego must always respect the freedom of others. Everyone must limit his own freedom by understanding the possibility of freedom in others, on condition that others behave in the same way towards him. This condition forms the basis of Fichte's political philosophy. Whenever man's freedom is not mutually respected, the authority of the state must intervene to enforce this respect. The state derives its legal foundation from the common will to safeguard man's basic right to freedom. Napoleon's infringement of this freedom aroused Fichte to heated protest in his *Reden an die deutsche Nation* (1808).

The thought of FRIEDRICH WILHELM JOSEPH SCHELLING (1775-1845) followed a different course. It can be divided into five separate periods which are not completely distinct from one another—the problems studied in each period are always a development from those considered in the preceding period. In the first period, Schelling's thought was closely geared to Fichte's doctrine of knowledge. The second period was his period of natural philosophy, the third that of his philosophy of identity, the fourth that of his philosophy of freedom and the fifth that of his religious philosophy. Schelling was precociously gifted as is witnessed by an enormous productivity in the first part of his life. His final period was one of silence, but not of diminished power of thought. During this period, he foresaw all the objections that Kierkegaard was later to make against idealism.

In his earliest works, Schelling's thought was entirely in accordance with that of Fichte. The absolute principle of all reality and all thought is the ego. The world proceeds from the ego and the infinite world is simply our creative mind in infinite productions and reproductions. But at quite an early stage in his life Schelling began to realize that he had an independent task of his own to fulfil. In Fichte's doctrine of knowledge, the whole emphasis was on free thought, that is, on the ego. The non-ego posited by the ego, however, remained obscure. Schelling set himself the task, in his natural philosophy, of examining this non-ego, the world of nature, within the framework of Fichte's doctrine of knowledge. In this, he was undoubtedly encouraged by the fact that all the positive natural sciences were at that time flourishing more than ever before. Within the framework of Fichte's thought which he had taken over, Schelling regarded nature simply as an unconscious product of the mind. It shows the laws according to which the mind works unconsciously. In a certain sense, it is a history of the mind, a history of its development and activity before it reaches consciousness. The outside world is open to us so that we may rediscover the history of our mind in it. Gradually, however, nature came to acquire more and more reality of its own in Schelling's thought, until it was no longer a question of nature being produced by the mind, but of the mind proceeding from nature. But this train of thought was not diametrically opposed to Fichte's ideas. According to Schelling's more mature view, the mind proceeded from nature as the conscious from the unconscious. Both the conscious and the unconscious were, for Schelling, forms in which the mind manifested itself, with the result that what he had to say about the mind proceeding from nature applied only to the conscious mind. Nature was a process of evolution from which the conscious mind proceeded, gradually coming to consciousness of itself and recognizing itself in unconscious nature.

These ideas are typical of Schelling's thought at the transition stage between the second and the third periods of his philosophy. In his philosophy of identity, the mind (the ego) and nature (the world) are placed opposite to each other as equals, as the ideal and the real or the subject and the object. They are identical in their origin, divinity, which is absolute identity or absolute indifferentiation. They both proceed from this absolute and indifferentiated identity and, in so doing, come to be opposite to each other, not in complete separateness, but in a mutual involvement which is apparent both in the forms of the mind and in the phenomena of nature. Nature proceeds from the unconscious divinity in increasingly higher forms— matter, movement, life, the world system and man. In nature's emanation from divinity, reason also comes to itself in increasingly higher forms—knowledge, morality, art, history and the state. Unlike Fichte, but in keeping with certain ideas from Kant's *Critique of Judgement,* Schelling placed art above morality.

Schelling's philosophy of freedom of his fourth period was inspired by religion. He was clearly influenced by neo-Platonism and by Jakob Böhme. The absolute of this period is no longer indifferentiated identity, but God as pure spirit. This pure spirit is a thinking activity. In this thinking, it produces its own spiritual image which is objectivized in the multiplicity of ideas. The great question here is, how does creation proceed from the divine, the finite from the infinite, the temporal from the eternal and the sensory from the spiritual? This cannot take place by means of a gradual development. It can only be brought about by a falling away from God. The finite is a falling away from the infinite by virtue of freedom. Freedom is therefore no longer the principle of all morality, but the principle of sin. The finite ego's placing of itself opposite to the infinite God is the principle of all evil. But the ego, which has fallen away from God by its free self-determination, is able to return again to God by knowledge, art and morality. Indeed, a return to God is the ultimate aim of all things and of the whole process of the world. Moreover, the ultimate cause of this falling away is to be found in God himself, in whom there is not only light, but also darkness. This darkness affects man as evil and man's salvation is to be found in his overcoming of this evil—

everything that lives must pass through the fire of contradiction.

Schelling elaborated this religious philosophy along more
positive lines in his fifth period. His work during this period
was at the same time accompanied by a controversy with Hegel
and by profound speculation about the meaning of experience.
He was at this time also deeply concerned with mythology
and the Christian revelation, which came to assume an increasingly central position in his thought. He became more
and more convinced that there was a reality that was not
dependent on thought. His ideas were, however, far from
systematic, and they became so difficult to follow during his
last years in Berlin, from 1814 onwards, that his lectures were
no longer attended. He died, a lonely and forgotten man, in
Bad Ragaz in Switzerland.

Schelling lived at the time of the German romantic movement and was closely associated with it. While he was a
student at Tübingen, he became friendly with Hegel and
Hölderlin and at Jena he formed part of a circle which included
Novalis and Friedrich von Schlegel. Schiller had come under
the influence of Kant even before this time, but Schelling,
with his great interest in the arts, had more contact with poets
and artists that with any other philosopher, with the result that
he even had a considerable influence on Goethe.

There was also important contact between the philosophy
of idealism and theology. In Schelling and Hegel especially,
theological ideas occur frequently and both of these philosophers had a powerful influence on theology. FRIEDRICH
SCHLEIERMACHER (1768-1843) was influenced on the one hand
by idealism and on the other by Herder's and Jacobi's philosophy of feeling. He was above all concerned with the essence
of the religious. He believed that this was to be found in feeling
as a specific function, distinct from thought and morality and
consequently, unlike Kant, he upheld the distinctive nature of

the religious. Religion, for Schleiermacher, was the feeling of complete dependence on the Absolute, but religion had no need to ask what this Absolute was in itself—it was sufficient simply to recognize it.

Idealism was most fully developed by GEORG WILHELM FRIEDRICH HEGEL (1770-1831) who, although he was five years older than Schelling, achieved fame later. In the latter period of his life, Hegel's reputation completely overshadowed that of Schelling. He succeeded Fichte as professor in Berlin in 1818 and his lectures received exceptional applause. As a young man, he was powerfully influenced by Fichte and even more by Schelling. Gradually, however, he began to dissociate himself more and more from their ideas and to formulate his own thoughts. These were clearly expressed in his *Phänomenologie des Geistes* (*Phenomenology of Spirit*, 1807) and his later works, the *Wissenschaft der Logik* (*Science of Logic*, 1812-6), the *Encyclopädie der philosophischen Wissenschaften* (*Encyclopedia of the Philosophical Sciences*, 1817), which Hegel wrote as a manual of instruction in philosophy and which provides the only full exposition of his thought, and finally the *Rechtsphilosophie* (*Philosophy of Right*, 1821). On 14 November 1831, he died of cholera in Berlin.

Hegel attempted to find the absolute in the relative. The absolute is the mind or spirit, but the mind is externalized in nature, in order to come to consciousness of itself. The mind is essentially the idea, that is, thought. This thought comes to itself in the history of man. Thus mankind shares in the absolute idea which is divinity. The thinking idea is essentially activity and movement. But this movement is not in a straight line. It takes place in constantly renewed movements and countermovements and a new movement grows out of this thesis and antithesis which contains within itself the two previous movements as a synthesis on a higher level. This process, which takes place according to the laws of reason, was called by Hegel the dialectic. Above all, the axiom, the real is the rational and the rational is the real, applies. The movement of the mind, and therefore the movement of nature and of history, is necessarily included in this dialectical movement.

In accordance with this movement, Hegel divided philosophy into three main parts. These divisions, which are reminiscent of the late Greek classification of philosophy into logic, physics and ethics, are logic, nature and spirit. Logic is the science of the idea in itself. The philosophy of nature is the science of the idea in its being different, that is, in its externalization in nature. The philosophy of spirit is the science of the idea which returns to itself from its being different. The following outline of Hegel's philosophy is based on this plan and the structure of the *Encyclopedia*.

The first Hegelian division of philosophy, logic, includes three sub-divisions—the doctrine of being, the doctrine of essence and the doctrine of the concept. Logic begins with the most general, and hence the most empty concept, being. In so far as being (as thesis) is given no more accurate definition, it is identical with nothing (as antithesis). But being is not undefined and neither is nothing, therefore there is only becoming (as synthesis). In becoming, being and nothing are united on a higher level (*aufgehoben*). Becoming is not what it will be, but neither is it purely nothing. Hegel always saw being in the light of its possible definition as quality, which was contrasted with quantity. In measure, in the sense of proportion or harmony, the two come together in synthesis.

Essence is lasting and unchangeable being. Reflection about essence in itself produces the fundamental principles of identity, contradiction and sufficient reason. Essence appears outwardly as the phenomenon and existence is not behind the phenomenon, it is the phenomenon. Essence and phenomenon thus form a unity in reality, the unity of the inward and the outward.

If being externalizes itself in essence, it returns to itself in the concept. The concept is subjective only as concept, judgement and decision. In contrast, the concept is objective in the forms of mechanical regulation, chemical combination and purposiveness. The absolute concept or the idea as synthesis results from the encounter between the subjective and the objective concept. This synthesis becomes life only when the subjective and the objective penetrate each other. In contrast, there is knowledge, in which the objective is assimilated into the subjective in a different way. When life and knowing come together at a higher level as a unity, the absolute idea is attained. This absolute idea is the pure form of the concept, which regards its content as itself.

In the Hegelian philosophy of nature, the idea is considered in its outward form. Nature is, however, still idea and, in its highest form (man), the idea returns to itself. Hegel divided his philosophy of nature, like his logic, into three parts—mechanics, physics and organic physics. Mechanics deals with matter and its movement in time and space. Physics deals with individual bodies as determined by our reflection with their physical and chemical laws. Physics, as thought-out nature, is contrasted with mechanics, as nature that is not thought-out. In organic physics, the third Hegelian division of nature, matter is revealed as inspired, that is, as the living, but not as the thinking idea.

Through nature, the idea or the spirit returns to itself. In this phase, spirit is first subjective, then objective and finally absolute. As subjective spirit, the mind comes to know itself. This development also includes three phases—anthropology, phenomenology and psychology. In anthropology, the mind comes to itself in the grasp of nature. In phenomenology, the mind gets to know itself in its difference from nature. In psychology, it recognizes itself as freedom that is involved with nature—first as theoretical spirit, then as practical spirit and finally as free spirit.

This brings us to the second stage—the objective spirit. The objective spirit is the absolute idea, appearing in the forms of human society and therefore, to some extent, externalized. It is revealed as law, morals and morality. In law, freedom is realized according to general laws and the objective spirit is revealed in its outward aspect, which is contrasted with the inward aspect of morals. Here it is simply a matter of conscience, of free moral decision on the part of the subjective will. The outward aspect of legality and the inward aspect of morals are raised to a higher level and become one in the synthesis of morality, which is the community as the social form of the free will. This community is first the family, then society and finally the state. The family, based on monogamous marriage, is the nucleus of society in which two people are merged into a higher unity so as to produce others for society. In contrast with the close bond of marriage, society is a loose multiplicity of persons which is held together only by common needs. The unity of the family and the multiplicity of society come together at a higher level in the state, which is the highest form of morality and the culminating point of the objective spirit.

The idea comes to itself completely as absolute spirit, which forms the synthesis of the subjective and the objective spirit. The antitheses between subject and object, thinking and being, are raised to a higher level and cancelled out in absolute spirit. Since it is also essentially movement, the absolute spirit also reveals a synthetic development. It is revealed first as art, then as religion and finally as philosophy. Art seizes the idea in sensory contemplation as an object that vividly expresses the unity of idea and phenomenon. It is revealed first in the symbolism of the eastern people, in which form predominates. In contrast, the art of classical antiquity preserves a balance between the inward spirit and the outward spirit. In the last stage of art, romanticism, the inward aspect is completely predominant over the form.

Religion, the second stage of the absolute spirit, does not regard the religious idea as an external object, but receives the object into the mind. It does, however, remain in front of the religious image and regards this image as reality. The first form of religion is the natural religion of the eastern people. The second form is the religion of subjectivity as that of the Jews, the Greeks and the Romans. The highest form of religion is Christianity, the absolute religion of truth and freedom. It is therefore clear that Hegel reduced religion entirely to thought, that is, to the self-development of the idea.

Philosophy is the unity of art and religion, in which both are raised to a higher level. It is in philosophy that the absolute spirit at last comes to a complete understanding of itself. The content of philosophy is not different from that of religion, but what is known in religion as image is understood in philosophy as idea. The history of philosophy is the history of the idea coming to itself. In this history, we see the dialectical development ultimately attaining its last and highest phase and coming to its close (with Hegel). Every philosophical system corresponds to a category of thought, but against every category another can always be set. Thus we see, in the history of philosophy, one system contrasted with another and this is followed by both systems being raised to a higher level and united in a synthesis. For example, the Ionian natural philosophers expressed the category of being. The Eleatics then affirmed the opposite category of nothing. Finally, Heraclitus proposed the synthesis in his fundamental category of becoming. Thus, the development of philosophy follows a necessary course. Every system has its own truth and all truth is ultimately included in the final synthesis, Hegel's dialectic, in which the human mind and, in it, the divine, comes to perfect self-knowledge and in which the divine idea finally comes to itself after many wanderings.

In view of the way in which Hegel himself worked it out

and the influence that it exerted, something must be said here about Hegel's view of the state. For Hegel, the state was the supreme embodiment of the moral idea. Because the idea is divine, the state is 'God present on earth' and the history of states is the 'course of God in the world'. As the appearance of God, the state is the perfectly rational and the laws of the state are the expression of pure reason—'the laws of the state are not fortuitous, they are reason itself'. Because it is the highest realization of the reasonable idea, the state is also the unconditional aim in itself. The state is not for the citizens—the citizens are there for the state, so that the moral idea may be fulfilled in the state. The state therefore has supreme rights with regard to individuals. Its laws are always valid and the individual conscience has no rights with regard to the state's laws.

This does not mean that Hegel held that the individual had no intrinsic dignity and was not an end in himself. For him, man's highest task was to serve the idea and, seeing this idea realized in the state, he believed that man was in fact realizing himself in serving the state. There was therefore, in Hegel's political philosophy, no antithesis between personal rights and the rights of the state. In his view, the rational laws of the state promoted the freedom of the citizen of the state and, by keeping these laws, the citizen realized his own freedom.

Hegel's philosophy had an enormous influence, but Hegelian thought very soon branched off into very different directions. Even Hegel's own disciples formed themselves into three distinct groups. The right wing interpreted his philosophy in a theistic sense and regarded it as a powerful support for orthodox Protestantism, while regarding it in the political sense as upholding the prevailing view of the state. The centre group merged Christian dogma into the concept and interpreted Hegel pantheistically. The work of both these groups was very important in spreading and interpreting Hegel's teaching. The left wing of so-called young Hegelians, however, was much more important both philosophically and politically. This group interpreted Hegel very freely. Its members took over his dialectical method and applied it especially to social questions, and in so doing they came to very different political conclusions from Hegel himself. I shall return to some of these left-wing Hegelians—Feuerbach, Marx and Engels—later. Russian Hegelianism, which played a leading part in the intellectual preparation for the Russian revolution, was another branch of this left-wing group.

ARTHUR SCHOPENHAUER (1788–1860) occupied an entirely separate position in the history of idealism. He remained outside the life of the university, which no doubt accounts for his bitterness towards university philosophy. His most important work was *Die Welt as Wille und Vorstellung (The World as Will and Idea, 1819)*. In this, Schopenhauer affirmed, not the primacy of reason, but the primacy of the will and, in connection with this, a pessimistic view of world renunciation as against the other idealists' optimistic acceptance of life. Schopenhauer was also the first western philosopher to be strongly influenced by Indian philosophy.

Schopenhauer was convinced that experience can take us no farther than the phenomenon. The world is simply an idea ot the thinking subject, an idea which is determined by our way of knowing. The possibility of the outside world is given by the *a priori* forms of time and space. By means of the principle of causality, our intellect links the impressions of our senses with external causes. But the way of thought is not the only path along which we can approach the ground of reality. It is not even the best path, for this is in fact the way of the will.

Man discovers the will in himself as the driving force which rises from the unconscious into the conscious mind. The will is the most inward force, becoming external as the lower or inferior will in the body, which is the object of sensory knowledge, and as the higher or superior will in thought, which is the object of itself and which calls to mind the idea of the world. The will is not simply the driving force in us—it is the driving force in the entire world. The world will also develops from the unconscious to the conscious and every stage of this development has its own special externalization— first the inorganic world, then the world of plants and finally the world of animals. In the world of man, the will comes to self-consciousness.

The will thus shows itself as the absolute ground of the world, as the blind will to exist which gradually comes to itself. This fundamental principle is not rational. It is above all irrational—the will to exist is both aimless and unfathomable and the man who comes to understand this regards his own life as meaningless. Existence does not justify itself—it is, on the contrary, evil as such. Does not sorrow, after all, always and everywhere far exceed happiness in the world?

There is therefore only one possible ethical course—to renounce existence. In so choosing, there are two possibilities —either to forget existence or to overcome it by completely renouncing the world. Forgetting existence can only be temporary and is therefore only a stupefaction and not a cure. Art makes us capable of forgetting existence from time to time, but at the same time makes us, after this period of forget-fulness, return all the more painfully again to life. Only a moral renunication of life and the world can enable us permanently to overcome existence. This renunciation is accomplished by asceticism, which enables us to maintain a distance from every-thing and finally to subdue the will so that we want nothing more. At this stage, we sink into nothing, Nirvana, the only state in which we can find peace.

The will which upholds life is bad. Only the will which renounces life is good. The supreme virtue is compassion, because, with this virtue, we take the passion or suffering of others upon ourselves and allow ourselves to become pervaded with the evil of existence. Compassion is at the root of the two main virtues, justice and love. Justice is a negative virtue which tries to avert evil. Love is a positive virtue which tries to help others. Compassion thus leads us to closer union with others and therefore closer to the root from which we have all sprung and in which we shall all go under again. To return with others to unconsciousness is the principle of morality.

In his recognition of the importance of suffering, the passions, the will and the irrational, Schopenhauer anticipated the philosophers of a later period, but these later thinkers also broke with idealism, to which Schopenhauer, in his own strange way, remained faithful. But, in order to understand how this later philosophy came about, it is first necessary to consider a tradition in German thought which has so far remained very much in the background—the school of realistically orientated metaphysics. In the first half of the nineteenth century, this was entirely overshadowed by idealism and, in the second half, by positivism. The philosophers of this school were very different from each other. Herbart and Lotze were inspired by Kant, whom they interpreted as realistically as possible, Bolzano was a realist in the Aristotelian spirit and Fechner took as his point of departure the problem of the relationship between the body and the soul.

JOHANN FRIEDRICH HERBART (1776–1841) was in turn a professor at Göttingen, Königsberg and finally at Göttingen again. His most important works were *Hauptpunkte der Metaphysik* (1806–8), *Allgemeine praktische Philosophie* (1808) and *Allgemeine Metaphysik* (1828–9). His most important contributions were made in the fields of psychology and education. In philosophy, he tended, with his successor Lotze and indeed, with his predecessor Kant, to regard the world of experience as a world of phenomena, but he also strove above all to describe the concrete content of these phenomena and to explain them. Phenomena, in Herbart's opinion, necessarily pointed to an objective reality. In the world of phenomena, contradiction frequently prevails, but contradiction is not acceptable to reality. The systematic study of phenomena, which teaches us to understand these as the expression of reality, provides us with the possibility of eliminating this contradiction. To do this, Herbart accepted the existence of a multiplicity of single, unchangeable and not extended elements of reality, which he called *Realen,* and explained all the multiplicity, change and diversity of phenomena as a combination of these *Realen.* Herbart also saw psychic life as a conflict of ideas combining with each other and trying to supplant each other. He also traced feeling and desire back to ideas and insisted that, as no idea ever entirely disappeared, it was of great importance in education to impart as many ideas as possible, in other words, to provide positive knowledge.

HERMANN LOTZE (1817–81), whose most important work was *Mikrokosmos* (1856–64), followed Herbart in 1844 as professor at Göttingen. He elaborated Herbart's doctrine of the *Realen* into a theory of monads in the spirit of Leibniz. The whole of reality consists of monads which are intimately related to each other. At the summit of this system of relationships is God. Philosophy is not only concerned with the real world of monads, it is also concerned with the values which transcend this world. The values form a special realm of constant validity —they *are* not, but are *valid.* It is only in God, who is not only the ground of the world, but also the supreme value from which all other values proceed, that the spheres of reality and value coincide. Lotze's philosophy of values had a great influence on philosophy at the end of the nineteenth century.

BERNHARD BOLZANO (1781–1848), who was a professor in Prague from 1805 until 1819 and whose most important work was his *Wissenschaftslehre* (1837), criticized Kant and Hegel very sharply. His aim was to return to an objective and realistic philosophy. His starting-point was Aristotle, although even in his case there is a noticeable influence from Leibniz. Truth is not dependent on man who thinks it, but is true in itself and precedes all human knowledge. Metaphysical truth is, however, accessible to thought. The existence of God and the immortality of the soul are truths which can be rationally proved. There is an important distinction between subjective and objective judgement. Objective judgement corresponds to the truth as such and is independent of all human thought—it is the object of logic. Subjective judgement, on the other hand, is the judgement that takes place in the psychical process and is the object of psychology. In some of his ideas, Bolzano already anticipated the phenomenology of Husserl.

GUSTAV THEODOR FECHNER (1801–87), who wrote, among other things, *Die Elemente der Psychophysik* (1860) and was himself a physicist, was particularly concerned with problems of psychophysical interaction. Body and soul are two different ways of expressing the same reality, so that it is possible to know the soul from the physical phenomena of the body. Since these phenomena are measurable, it is also possible to gain a knowledge of the soul that can be formulated mathematically. Thus Fechner, together with Herbart, was in a sense a pioneer of modern experimental psychology. Man is not the only reality—he is part of the earth. His body is part of the material process of the earth and his soul is part of the soul of the earth, which is itself also part of the universal spirit, or the soul of the universe. These speculations led Fechner to oppose Kant, who had no understanding of all this.

In the second half of the nineteenth century, materialism began to play a part in German philosophy. LUDWIG FEUERBACH (1804–72), a disciple of Hegel, gave German materialism its first impulse. The only thing that is is nature. Man is a being of nature and his striving is a natural urge to live. This striving takes priority over knowledge, as knowledge is only a means of satisfying our strivings. Human happiness is to be found in this satisfaction and morality is simply man's striving towards this happiness, which can only be achieved in this world. The adage 'be satisfied with this world' applies both to knowledge and to action. Thus religion and metaphysics must both be rejected—they are only transpositions of strivings which are not fulfilled in this world. Although the only principle of morality is the urge for happiness, this does not mean that egoism should be the guide for morality. My fellow-men form as real a part of this world as I do and the I-thou relationship in fact constitutes the most essential element of our being men, so that the happiness of my fellow-man affects me as much as my own happiness. The more fellow-men I can include in my urge for happiness, the greater is my morality. Morality, however, has no origin of its own apart from the knowledge of experience—it is based on experience. Experience teaches us that we must, in our urge for happiness, take into account our fellows' urge for happiness. In this way, ethics also falls within the naturalist framework and everything is reduced to the urge to live.

As Feuerbach recognized the distinctive nature of life as against dead matter, it is possible, and perhaps preferable, to speak of naturalism in his case rather than of materialism in the strict sense. Very soon, however, a completely materialist philosophy was developed by those who succeeded him. These thinkers had recourse to the development of natural science which, they believed, would eventually make it possible for man to explain the whole of reality, including the most sublime expressions of the mind, from material forces. The great significance of nineteenth century German materialism, which was constructed on the foundations laid by the French materialists of the previous century, was that it forced men to consider the irreducible characteristics of the spiritual. The reaction that it provoked was more important to philosophy than its own active contribution. This reaction went back to Kant, because it was realized that even a full explanation of the known would not necessarily imply an explanation of knowing.

Although 'natural scientific' materialism had a wide influence, the influence of dialectical materialism went much deeper. KARL MARX (1818–83) was won over to the philosophy of Hegel in Berlin and soon occupied a very special place on the left wing of the Hegelians. He was exiled from Prussia and thereafter lived in Paris, Brussels and London. Marx succeeded in welding philosophical and scientific thought into a single whole with social and political thought. The writings of the young Marx are very important for an understanding of the philosophical assumptions that underlie this entirety of thought and action. This period closed with the publication in 1848 of the *Communist Manifesto*, which Marx wrote in collaboration with Engels. Marx himself regarded *Das Kapital* (Part I, 1867; the two succeeding parts were published posthumously) as his main work. Marx was deeply influenced by Hegel, from whom he took over, among other things, the dialectical method and the conviction that philosophy, history and society were very closely connected, and Feuerbach, to whom he owed his tendency to explain the spiritual from the material and to direct all his attention to man living in the community. The French communists, Saint-Simon and Proudhon, also influenced him considerably.

Marx succeeded in making a very close connection between economics and philosophy in his thought. He did not elaborate his theory simply for its own sake—it was to be put to use. Neither knowledge nor pure will, but action had priority in Marx's case—'the philosophers have only explained the world in various ways. Our task is to change it'. In Marx's view, human life was entirely determined by economic relationships. All the spiritual activities of mankind—science, art, religion, morality, law and politics—were the result of these relationships, which were historically determined. There were originally no classes in primitive society, but these came about with specialization of labour and the introduction of property. This led to the emergence of the property-owning class, the capitalists, and the unpropertied class, the proletariat. Marx was convinced that the struggle between these two classes would by natural determinism become increasingly more violent until it was ultimately decided by a revolution in which the proletariat would seize power from the capitalist class. After an initial period of transition—the dictatorship of the proletariat—the age of classless society would dawn. In this society, the ownership of the means of production would be in the hands of the whole community, in other words, the state. This state, however, would no longer be the national state, but the world community of nations. This world state of the future would mark the end of history—the classless and unpropertied society of the primitive state and the specialized means of production of the capitalist period would be united in it in a higher synthesis.

Marx combined a deep interest in philosophy, largely inspired by Hegel and Feuerbach, with a great social concern which was the driving force for his prophetic inspiration and his enormous output of work. His materialism went deeper than that of the 'natural scientific' materialists. As with Feuerbach, man was determined by his nature, but, for Marx, nature was society. He saw it as his task to point out the direction in which history was necessarily moving, since this necessary movement was made by men themselves. The fact that the individual was thus determined did not preclude freedom, since freedom was, in Marx's view, simply an awareness of one's own determined state. Marx turned to the proletariat, the class without property, because this was the class of the future, the class with which history would make progress. The property-owning class was simply reactionary. Marx made an interesting analysis of the factors of progress and reaction. One of the most important instruments of the reactionary bourgeoisie was, in his opinion, religion, the 'opium of the people'. Religion could therefore have no meaning at all for the proletariat or for the communist state of the future. Although it could have no religion, the proletariat could, however, have philosophy, science, art, morality, law and politics. But, because all spiritual activities were determined by social relationships, all these expressions of the human mind and spirit were of an entirely different kind in the case of the proletariat—dialectical materialism was the only possible proletarian philosophy, the policy of the communist party was the only possible proletarian policy and, similarly, science, art, morality and law were all determined, as far as their content was concerned, by the class that produced them and supported them.

Marx always worked in close collaboration with FRIEDRICH ENGELS (1820-95). Their views were in general very similar and, as research into the differences between their ideas has so far not yielded any firm results, it is not possible to deal separately with Engels here. The philosophy of both Marx and Engels is usually referred to either as historical materialism, on the basis of the philosophy of history which they developed, or as dialectical materialism, on the basis of the method that they employed. Their work has above all had an enormous political influence, but it has also had quite a considerable influence on the sciences of history, sociology and economics and recently also on philosophy.

Marx and Engels wrote in conscious reaction against the bourgeois civilization that was brought about by the social conditions prevailing at the beginning of the industrial age. SÖREN KIERKEGAARD (1813-55), who, with the exception of a few journeys to Berlin, spent his whole life in Copenhagen,

G

also reacted violently against the bourgeoisie, but, in his case, the reaction was primarily against its absence of inward quality. The problem that preoccupied him was that of becoming a Christian. While he was a student of theology, he was won over to Hegel, but very soon turned against him, because Hegel allowed concrete existence to be lost in the generality of the idea. From arguing against Hegel, in his *Philosophical Fragments* (1844) and the *Postscript to the Philosophical Fragments* (1846) especially, Kierkegaard went on to develop his own view of existence. For Hegel, the existence of the individual was only an element in the development of the idea. For Kierkegaard, on the other hand, man was above all concerned with his own individual existence. Man must choose this existence in freedom, conscious of the irreducibility of his own individual distinctiveness. Existence is not an idea in the ordinary sense—it is an action that every man must perform for himself. No one can exist in my place. To exist is the act of distinctiveness that is irreducible in all dialectic. It is the concrete, individual existence in the world that determines itself but is at the same time determined by time and the world. In precisely this way, only man exists. God, the animals and things exist, but not in this distinctive way.

Although every existence is absolutely unique, it is possible to indicate certain special modes of existence, and Kierkegaard came back again and again to this question, dealing with it especially in his *Stages on Life's Way* (1845). He distinguished three forms of life—the aesthetic, the ethical and the religious. These three forms are not an extension of each other. One can only get from a lower to a higher form by a jump and it is always possible to fall back again from a higher form to a lower. The aesthete is the man who is interested in everything, but whom nothing touches. He is directed towards the outside world and is immersed in sensual and spiritual enjoyment, but he has no inward self and always seeks to avoid all fundamental decisions. The ethical man is the man who takes his inward self seriously. He does not live with concrete beings, like the aesthete, but endeavours to determine his attitude in the world in accordance with general guiding lines arising from his inward self. He is the man whose attitude towards himself and others is one of serious responsibility. Finally, there is the religious attitude to life. Kierkegaard distinguished two levels of religiousness—firstly, the religiousness which assumed nothing beyond human nature as such and in which man could discover his essential attitude towards the Eternal, an attitude of guilty nothingness, and secondly, the religiousness which far transcended the first and recognized Christ as God made man, the point at which time and eternity crossed and the Paradox which was the measure of every existence.

Kierkegaard stated the choice between aesthetic and ethical existence very clearly even in his first great work, *Either/Or* (1843). It is quite obvious here, as in all Kierkegaard's other works, how intimately related were his life and thought. This book was the result of his breaking off his engagement with Regina Olsen. What emerges with great clarity here is that to exist is to dare to make a choice that will determine one's life. Anyone who does not dare to choose does not exist in the real sense of the word. This in turn draws attention to the theme of real and unreal existence. The aesthete does not exist in the proper sense, but the ethical man does. Real existence takes place in subjectivity. It is not a question of objective reality or truth, but of a truth which is 'truth for me, an idea for which I wish to live and die'. In his later work, Kierkegaard gave more and more prominence to the meaning of religious existence.

Not only the breaking off of his engagement, but also his incurable melancholy and the secret which his father confided to him (a secret which has still not been fully unravelled) make Kierkegaard's life and work a struggle waged in extreme despair. He also had two different ways of writing. In his orations, he presented his Christian thoughts in a relatively simple manner. In his great works, on the other hand, he wrote experimentally—carrying certain points of view through to their extreme consequences, not because he himself shared these views, but because he wanted to see the truth emerge as a result of dialectical reasoning from these extremes.

What sharply distinguishes Kierkegaard from Hegel and the rationalists is his conviction of the inadequacy of reason. This conviction did not, however, lead him to neglect reason. On the contrary, he used it to its extreme limit, so that its ultimate failure was evident from itself. For Kierkegaard, then, the last word was always the paradox, seen not as an initial equalization of two opposites, but as a definitive equalization. Kierkegaard's paradox was therefore the absurd itself. Man is always coming up against the absurd. He does not live safely in the house of rationality, but in the harsh desolation of the absurd, in which he must in loneliness determine his existence by his own fundamental choice. Existence is a hazardous venture and man must take on all its risks if he wishes to exist in the real sense. His existential choice must also be repeated again and again— it is not simply made once and for all time. It confronts man again and again with his responsibility and challenges him to take his fate into his own hands. For the religious man, this means that he should, in recognition of the absurdity of existence, surrender his fate to God. Although every man suffers from the irreconcilability of time and eternity, the greatest burden falls on the Christian, who accepts, in Christ, the reconciliation of time and eternity and therefore the Paradox made man itself. Kierkegaard's conflict with the state Church was most clearly expressed in his book *The Moment* (1855), in which he argued that the official Christianity of the state Church was not true Christianity. Kierkegaard's diary, which gives an invaluable insight into his inner life, is also indispensable to anyone who wishes to understand his thought and work correctly.

I have discussed Kierkegaard here, under the German philosophers of the nineteenth century, because his philosophy was evolved partly in reaction against Hegel and because he heard Schelling when he was in Berlin. Otherwise, of course, he was an isolated figure and his work was conditioned by typically Danish circumstances. Kierkegaard reacted quite differently from Marx towards Hegel, but the two thinkers shared the common conviction that human existence was first and foremost an action. A similar view was also held by Nietzsche, although his philosophy was otherwise very far removed from all forms of either Christianity or communism.

In his life, FRIEDRICH NIETZSCHE (1844–1900) struggled, like Kierkegaard, with himself and the world. He studied classical philology at Leipzig University and was appointed professor at Basle in 1869. Ten years later, however, he had to give up his post because of poor health. From that time onwards, he was unable to settle anywhere in peace and wandered restlessly from place to place. His most important works appeared during this time. It is possible to distinguish three separate periods in his written work. The first was inspired by Greek tragedy, the pessimism of Schopenhauer and the music of Richard Wagner. In this period, his view of life was predominantly pessimistic. Art provided a means of flight from reality. In his first work, Nietzsche contrasted Dionysian passion with Apollonian rationality. In the second period, he had a predominantly positivist view of life—inspiration was subordinate to critical analysis of all expressions of the mind. The third period opened with the publication of *Also sprach Zarathustra* (*Thus Spoke Zarathustra*, 1883–5), in which Nietzsche set out his attitude of assent to life. In other works which he wrote at this time, Nietzsche criticized various other attitudes towards life and especially the Christian attitude. He also made many notes at this period for a final work, *Der Wille zur Macht, eine Umwertung aller Werte* (*The Will to Power*).

I shall not attempt, in this brief outline of Nietzsche's thought, to define accurately the different periods of his activity—the divisions between them are, in any case, not sharp—but simply to throw some light on his philosophy as a whole. Nietzsche was the philosopher of the vital passions. For him, the passions were the driving force in man and the spiritual was a superstructure above the life of passion. This super-structure could be in harmony with the life of passion, but it was generally in conflict with it. The passions all presented themselves, Nietzsche believed, as spirit because they were too weak to lead their own life, but as spirit they were a perversion of the life of passion. Nietzsche based his distinction between the morality of the slaves and that of the masters on this anti-thesis between the passions and the spirit. The master lives an untrammelled life of passion and does not seek refuge behind the excuses of the spirit. The slave, on the other hand, lacking the freedom to realize his passions in life, transforms these passions into spirit and thus evolves the morality which allows the spirit to dominate the passions. The great mass of slaves attempts to subordinate the smaller élite of masters by means of this morality. Nowhere has this been more successful than in Christianity.

In this context, Nietzsche asked himself what values really were. His answer was that a value was anything that served life. In Nietzsche's view, then, values were not absolute norms. The life passion itself projects the values that it needs and the values that are chosen depend on the direction of the passion. If this passion moves in an ascending line, it will produce the noble values that are characteristic of the master. If, on the other hand, it moves in a descending line, it will evolve the base values that characterize the morality of the slave. Everything, in Nietzsche's view, came down to the will to power, but not power in the sense of brutal domination by violence, but power as the superiority of the man who lives truly. In such a man, the spirit is not in conflict with the life of passion, but in its service.

The ideal man is Nietzsche's *Ubermensch*, in whom the will to power leads to complete control of the world. This control can only be acquired, however, in suffering. Only the man who has suffered greatly can think and only the thinker can really be a master. History finds its fulfilment in the *Ubermensch*, but every fulfilment demands a new beginning. Thus, everything returns again in history in an eternal cycle. As soon as history is fulfilled, everything commences again from the beginning and happens again in precisely the same way.

Nietzsche was even less systematic than Kierkegaard. His ideas were frequently contradictory. The negative element was much more fully worked out than the positive. 'God is dead'—this conviction underlay the whole of Nietzsche's philosophy and gave it its great power. The death of God has caused a great void which must at all costs be filled or life is not worth living, and the world will be engulfed in a nihilism which is coming closer all the time. Nietzsche did all his work under enormous psychological pressure to which he eventually succumbed, becoming completely insane at the beginning of 1889. His work, like Kierkegaard's, was a constant questioning, in which the answer was less important than the penetrating way in which the question was asked. Kierkegaard and Nietzsche were, in their questioning philosophy, the great exceptions of their age, but they were, at the same time, the pioneers of an entirely new way of thinking.

2. *French Philosophy*

At the beginning of the nineteenth century, French philosophy shows very many variations. The tradition of Condillac was continued by the *idéologues*, so called because they were above all concerned with the problem of the origin of knowledge. These philosophers tended gradually to abandon Condillac's reduction of all conscious thought to the knowledge of the senses. On the one hand, more and more attention was devoted to the physiological basis of the knowledge of the senses and, on the other, it was realized with increasing clarity that all knowledge of the mind could not be reduced to the senses alone. The problem of the unity of the ego also became more and more central.

The work of FRANÇOIS PIERRE MAINE DE BIRAN (1776–1824) played an important part in this development. Maine de Biran was born in Bergerac, where he later became *sous-préfet*. Later still, as deputy for Bergerac, he moved to Paris, remaining there until his death and returning to Bergerac and his family only during the vacations. He never held a chair of philosophy —all his philosophical works were produced in the midst of political activity. He published very little himself, his most important work being his *Mémoire sur l'influence de l'habitude sur la faculté de penser* (1803). His literary legacy, however, included a great number of studies in various stages of completion (1824), an important diary, the *Journal intime*, and his correspondence with many of the leading scientists of his day, including Ampére. Many of the studies that he left behind deal with various philosophers and reveal a deep and intimate knowledge of the thought of the past and of his own time.

Maine de Biran took inner experience as his point of departure. He was troubled and disturbed by the antithesis between the will and feeling. Our feelings are always in a state of movement—we are unable to hold on to them and we are even less able to invoke them. Where, then, is the unity of the ego? Am I my will or am I my feelings, which are always evading my grasp? This question led Maine de Biran to make a distinction between the passive and the active elements in man's conduct. Our impressions may be passive, in which case they are feelings or sensations, or they may be active, in which case they are perceptions. This distinction is intimately connected with mobility. Our impressions are more active when our organism is more mobile. Thus, our sense of touch is, for example, subject to passive impressions such as those of pain and heat, but it is, on the other hand, extremely active when our hand touches an object. Consciousness occurs only with active impressions; the purely passive impressions do not in themselves lead to consciousness. Consciousness always presupposes a duality. I am absorbed in my sensations, but, in my perceptions, what I experience is first of all the sense's will to move and secondly the object's resistance. Thus, the same experience reveals to me both the reality of the ego in the will and the reality of the outside world in the resistance of the object. It is the feeling of effort that puts me in touch with reality—there is no activity without effort, even though this may be only the slightest movement of the muscles, and there is no ego and no resistance without activity and consequently no revelation of the outside world.

The importance of the antithesis between passive feelings and active perceptions is clear from an analysis of habit. Feelings that are purely habitual become less acute. Habitual perceptions, on the other hand, become more acute. There is, for example, a great difference between hearing and listening and between seeing and looking. Knowledge always presupposes an active element. Thought itself is activity *par excellence*. The will is the basis of this difference between the passive and the active elements. All consciousness comes from the experience of the will in effort. This is *le fait primitif*—'Our point of departure is the simplest and most certain knowledge which our mind can acquire, without which no other knowledge is possible and by which all other knowledge is made possible'. This point of

departure is therefore effort, as revealed in the slightest movement of the muscles. Through effort, the ego gets to know
itself directly as a supracorporeal force which causes the movement of the muscles. Here then, effort does not mean trouble,
pains or endeavour, but the setting in motion of the experience
of the self.

The ego gets to know itself as cause. It has no direct intuition
of itself and can only get to know itself by the roundabout
route of effort. In this way, it comes directly to the idea of the
duality of reality. It is a non-material force, but it encounters
material resistance. Two important conclusions may be drawn
from this. Firstly, the ego is a force and not a substance in the
sense of a substratum, as Descartes regarded it. Secondly, it is
cause. The concept cause can never be found in the outside
world. It can only be traced back to inner experience, in which
I myself, in my effort, am the cause. The physical concept of
causality is an externalization of this inner concept of cause
which cannot be separated from experience.

For Maine de Biran, the great error of modern thinking was
the representation of this inner reality according to the model
of outward reality. The truth was, in his opinion, quite the
reverse—our idea of outward reality can only be based on our
experience and understanding of inner reality. This does away
with the dualism that leads us either to deny outward reality
or to accept materialism. Recognition of the duality of reality
in the experience of effort and resistance preserves us from
the dualism of Descartes, the acceptance of inner and outward
reality as two distinct and irreducible forms existing separately
side by side.

With the knowledge of the ego in the *fait primitif*, we at the
same time receive knowledge of all the fundamental concepts
—being, substance, cause, unity and identity. Reflection can
remove the vagueness of these concepts as contained in the *fait
primitif* and give us a much clearer understanding of them

These concepts are the condition for all thought and all knowledge. They are not innate, as Descartes believed them to be, but come about implicitly with the concept of experience of the ego and are developed from this by thought.

But how can these concepts have universal and absolute validity if they come from the ego? This question led Maine de Biran to make a distinction in thought. All knowledge is dependent on my experience of the *fait primitif*. But this experience of the ego is connected with another principle that is an essential part of our nature—the principle of faith. The individual concepts that are developed from the ego are recognized by faith as universal and absolute concepts. Thus faith forms a spiritual sphere above the sphere of the soul, that is, the sphere in which the ego discovers itself in effort. Maine de Biran was not using the word faith here in a religious sense, but in the sense of another form of thought which includes the individual among the universal and absolute concepts and exists besides knowledge, which always relates to individual experience.

Further reflection, however, led Maine de Biran to the idea of religion. His psychology enabled him to distinguish two states of the ego—a purely affective state and a state of inner contradiction. The affective state of the ego is in fact situated below the threshold which marks the real beginning of the ego, because this state is one of pure passivity, the state in which we are actuated by our feelings. The ego only properly appears when the will comes into play and thus brings about the antithesis between the passive feelings and the active perceptions. The ego is therefore always in conflict which cannot be avoided if we wish to be ourselves and which at the same time prevents us from being ourselves entirely. All we can do is to endure this inner conflict, since it is only increased by our annoyance about it.

But, just as there is an affective state of the ego which is situated below the real ego, so too is there a religious state which transcends the real ego. If thought is activity *par excellence*, taking place in continuous antithesis to our feelings which are not subject to thought, there is in man an even higher faculty which is open to the Infinite, to God. This faculty is neither activity nor pure passivity. It is the spirit's becoming one with God. The spirit here is purely receptive— it can only be open and cannot itself bring about the union with God. In this spiritual union with God, man achieves inner peace and unity, his life of feeling is brought to rest and his thought becomes passive in its openness to God. This is the third and the highest state of the ego, in which it does not avoid activity by sinking into feeling, but finds union with God and thus peace and unity by rising to the receptive cessation of thought.

This is Maine de Biran's life of the spirit (*vie de l'esprit*), just as the life of feeling is an animal life (*vie animale*) and the life of antithesis between the will and feeling is human life as such (*vie humaine*). Man is halfway between God and nature—in his spirit, he is related to God, in his feeling, with nature. By passively following the stream of his feelings, he can allow himself to become swallowed up by nature, but he can, on the other hand, be open to union with God. Plato understood this and Christianity has shown the full meaning of it. Thus, both the extreme states of man are states of passivity in which he loses his personality—in the first case to nature and in the second to God. But man can only find union with God when he has first found his personality in realizing himself in the tension between feeling and will. Only he who has first found his personality can give it up.

Maine de Biran's thought was overshadowed in the nineteenth century by that of Comte and by an eclectic philosophy that had recourse to Maine de Biran without really understanding his ideas. VICTOR COUSIN (1792-1867) published a number of his works without fully fathoming their meaning. Cousin advocated a spiritualistic philosophy containing the best elements of many different schools—Descartes and Maine de Biran, German idealism and the Scottish school. He himself called his philosophy, which was in no sense unified, eclecticism. Thanks to his prominent position, first in the University and later as Minister of Education, this eclecticism played an important part in French philosophy for a long time. Around the middle of the nineteenth century, it was the only movement which could equal positivism in influence.

The rapid social and political development of the first half of the nineteenth century caused a lively interest to be taken in social philosophy. Almost all the philosophers of this period were brought up against the problem of how a society that corresponded to the actual state of affairs was to be instituted and they attempted to solve it, some by going back to the past, but the majority by recognizing the new state of affairs and advocating the necessary reforms. The philosophy of Saint-Simon, Fourier and Proudhon, in many respects very closely related, was entirely concerned with social reform. The imminent industrial revolution was clearly foreseen by them.

CLAUDE-HENRI COMTE DE SAINT-SIMON (1760-1825) was confident that the growth of industry would bring about an improved social organization. The leaders of production would, he believed, replace the statesmen. Industry was applied science, and scholars and industrialists would have to direct production together and therefore govern the whole community of the state. They would assume the functions of the clergy and the nobility. Everyone would, in the future industrial society, have to work according to his gifts and be paid according to his work. A freely developing industry would itself create favourable conditions of work—it never occurred to Saint-Simon that there might be conflict between the employers and the workers. Going still further, Saint-Simon prophesied that the development of industry would break through national barriers and create the need for international consultation which would, in turn, promote peace between the nations. The growth of industry would lead not only to the unity of Europe, but also to the birth of a new Christianity, which would set aside all the outdated forms and live according to the morality of 'love one another'.

CHARLES FOURIER (1772-1837) took as his starting-point individual rather than collective work. Work must give satisfaction to the individual. Providence has established a harmonious order in lifeless and organic nature—it is only in the human community that order is lacking. Fourier sought therefore to find the principle of order. In nature, order came about when everything followed its tendencies. In human society, on the other hand, man was everywhere held in bondage. Work was a painful necessity for him and his greatest desire was to escape from it. Man's tendencies or aspirations had therefore to be given back their freedom, in which case he would once again find happiness in work. If work were attractive, productivity would increase and, with it, social welfare. To achieve this, it would be necessary for everyone to see the utility of his own work. This was, however, impossible in our complex society. Fourier therefore suggested the creation of small social units or 'phalanxes' which would provide entirely for their own needs and within which each individual could choose the work that was most congenial to him. In this way, order, happiness in work and productivity would go hand in hand.

JOSEPH PROUDHON (1809-65) took the idea of jusice as his point of departure. He was not, as a philosopher, concerned with pure speculation, but with a principle for action. This principle was, for him, justice, which was revealed in the balance of nature and which also had to control men's relations with one another. Proudhon aimed therefore to lead man back

THE NINETEENTH CENTURY   201

to nature. All men, being equal, had to work. Although capital should not yield interest, Proudhon believed that all property which was acquired by personal work without exploiting others was permissible.

The philosophy of AUGUSTE COMTE (1798-1857) was far more carefully thought out. In it, social and scientific order form a single whole. Comte wrote various works in which he set out his ideas, but the most important were his *Cours de philosophie positive* (1830-42) and his *Système de politique positive* (1851-4), each of which marked a definite phase in the development of his ideas. From the very beginning, Comte set himself two tasks—that of providing a philosophy of the sciences and that of providing a theoretical political science. Comte was preoccupied with the problem of how to consolidate the achievements of the French revolution and this was a problem with which he was particularly concerned, working, as he did, as Saint-Simon's secretary from 1817 until 1824. His earliest political ideas were consequently worked out along the lines of Saint-Simon's industrialism and he came therefore to understand the close connection between politics, economics and social conditions.

The basic principle of Comte's positivism is the acceptance of positive science as the starting point for philosophical thought and the rejection of inner experience as the source of any knowledge. Comte was not concerned here primarily with scientific facts as such, but with the knowledge which the development of positive science gives us of the human mind. We do not get to know the mind by inward reflection, but from the mind's works—the various positive sciences. The scientific method, the procedure that gives these sciences their hold on the world, enables us to see what the mind is. The mind would seem to be directed towards nature, not in order to contemplate it, but in order to form it in accordance with man's aims.

The methods that are applied in a science form the philosophy of that science. The whole body of these methods in the various sciences leads us to a general philosophy of science. This philosophy enables us to know what the mind is and what it should be by throwing light on the conditions for its success. This reflection about the scientific method is not the work of the scientist himself, but the work of the philosopher. In this way, despite Comte's rejection of inner experience as a source of knowledge, philosophy remains vitally important. It is also not a materialist philosophy because it is not orientated towards nature in itself, but a philosophy of the mind, because it aims to investigate the working of the mind in the methods of positive science. It is therefore both a philosophy of the mind and a philosophy of the sciences. But it must also be a philosphy of history, because the mind gradually discovers itself in the history of the sciences. This led Comte to ask two important questions—what stages do the various sciences pass through in order to reach maturity and what are these sciences?

Comte distinguished three stages in the development of every science—the theological stage, the metaphysical stage and the scientific or positive stage. The first stage explained phenomena from active causes which transcend the human level, but are still based on the human model—God or gods. The second stage kept to the same causes, but stripped them of their theological character and made abstract principles of them. Both the theological and the metaphysical stages worked with the concept of cause, which is derived from inner experience. This, however, must be rejected as a source of knowledge, with the result that the concept of causality must also be rejected and all that remains is the concept of relation. Thus the concept of the absolute loses all meaning, apart from its significance in connection with the principle of absolute relativity—'everything is relative; this is the only absolute principle'. The third stage is therefore the stage of relativity. In other words, it is the stage in which scientifically recognized relations form the only principle explaining positively established factuality. It is only in this final stage that there is any authentic science.

But, although all the sciences pass through these three stages, they do not pass through them simultaneously. The more complex a science is, the later it reaches the third stage. It is possible to follow this development if the sciences can successfully be arranged in their order of complexity.

Comte thus classified the sciences according to a plan in which each successive science presupposed the preceding one. According to Comte, there were therefore six fundamental sciences, to which all the others were subordinated as auxiliary or practical sciences. In Comte's classification then, the six basic sciences were mathematics, which was the technical aid to all the other sciences, astronomy, which added movement to mathematical relationship, physics, which also analysed matter and power, chemistry, which added the element of material change, biology, which introduced the phenomenon of life, and finally sociology, which examined the living being in its social relationships.

Comte excluded certain sciences from his classification. He did not, for example, include astrophysics, because the only knowledge that man had of the celestial bodies was of their movement, and he also excluded psychology, because he did not regard inner phenomena as scientific facts. He was also struck by the fact that, as the sciences became increasingly more complicated, their generality decreased. But for him the most important aspect of this classification was that it enables us to follow the growth of the positive mind in history. It was not until mathematics had become a positive science and had abandoned all causal explanations that astronomy could pursue the same course, later followed by physics, chemistry, biology and sociology. Comte regarded his work as the beginning of the third stage of history. One by one, the various sciences became positive sciences. The last, sociology, was raised to the level of a positive science by Comte himself.

Sociology and philosophy were the same for Comte. The sociologist investigated the specifically human in human phenomena. But what is this specifically human element, if it is not the world of inner perception? It is to be found in what is simply lacking in the life of animals—civilization. Man is different from the animal because he makes history. History is both tradition and progress. In the case of the animal, the same actions are repeated in the same way from generation to generation. In the case of man, on the other hand, such actions are certainly handed down from one generation to another, but these same actions are continuously being perfected. In this way, every man is united with all other men, both with his contemporaries and with men of the past and of the future. All men together form the one mankind (*l'Humanité*). Humanity has its own development and its own destiny which transcends the fate of individual men. In the strict sense, there are no individuals at the human level, since all men are united by many bonds and always form communities. The individual is an abstraction and only the community is a true reality. There are many forms of community, the smallest of these being the family. Families are therefore the smallest concrete realities from which all the larger communities are built. The human community is essentially historical—it is the history of the mind, that is to say, the mind itself.

Practice is preceded by theory and it was not until the science of sociology had been established that Comte could carry out his second task, that of providing a system of positive politics. Unlike his contemporaries, who were so uneasy and disturbed, Comte had a firm guide here in his doctrine of the three stages of scientific development. The guiding principles of positive politics are derived from the fact that mankind is entering the third stage of history. Since every policy provides society with its guiding principles, the first question to be asked is, what is a society or community? We can only speak of a community when human activity has a communal aim. Positive politics must therefore hold out a communal aim to humanity. Secondly, it must be remembered that a community can only have one of two aims—either conquest, in fighting against another community, or the subjection of nature to the well-being of the community.

Positive politics will confront society with its ultimate goal. The subjection of nature is the consequence of the development of the human mind and this development is ultimately a development of ideas, since everything that happens comes about as a result of ideas—'ideas control the world and overthrow it'. If a true community is to be formed, this work must be preceded by complete unity in conviction which must always be in accordance with the social situation, with the result that there can be no absolute norm. It is therefore, in the positive society, a question of subjecting nature to the well-being of the community and all power and energy must be directed towards the fulfilment of this aim. The direction of all power towards the fulfilment of the communal aim is the work of sociologists or philosophers, their expert scientific knowledge replacing the authority of the priests and rulers in the positive society. All leadership in society is to be pro-vided by such experts, so that all secular power is ultimately subjected to the power of the mind.

The working out of Comte's positive politics, however, took a course which many of his disciples, such as Taine, for example, regarded as a rupture in the development of Comte's teaching, with the result that only some of those who supported positivism wanted to follow this course. Comte was convinced that egoism was a deeply rooted, innate human characteristic.

He believed that, if the power of the mind was to prove itself superior to the powers of the world, human egoism would have to be overcome either by love or by altruism. But, since the truly human element was always to be found at the level of the community, the victory of altruism over egoism could only be achieved by the community, by mankind as a whole. This victory was, in Comte's view, the religion of humanity and the priesthood which had to ensure this victory was the corporation of sociologists or philosophers.

Comte's ideas did not change in the transition from the *Cours de philosophie positive* to the *Système de politique positive*, but his point of view did change. In the *Cours*, he was concerned with knowing as mankind's supreme function, whereas, in his *Système*, he was concerned with man's love for his fellow-men, because he was convinced that it was only love that could provide the motive power of knowledge. There is in fact no rupture between the two works, but a changed point of view and this change in his way of viewing things points to an inward change that had taken place in Comte himself, which was brought about, in part, by his relationship with Clotilde de Vaux, who taught him the meaning of personal love and of feeling. From this time onwards, Comte realized that he had to appeal to feeling if his ideas were to be carried through. He arranged his religious community according to the model of the Catholic Church, humanity taking the place of God and those who had prepared the way for the positive age replacing the saints. The positive religion had its own calendar, sacraments and veneration of the dead. Its members prayed and sacrificed themselves for the religious ideal. The individual was only there for humanity as a whole and for this reason the high priest of humanity was able to forbid the practice of those sciences that did not contribute to the well-being of humanity.

German philosophy had less influence on French thought

than is generally believed. Almost all the French idealists who had studied the works of Kant (and sometimes those of Fichte and Schelling as well) were more deeply influenced by Descartes than by Kant, although Kant's influence was very strong in the case of CHARLES RENOUVIER (1815-1903), whose philosophy was very important in France in the last quarter of the nineteenth century.

Three separate themes are present in Renouvier's philosophy. These themes do not form a unity. They are the impossibility of the infinite reality, the fundamental significance of freedom and the phenomenal and relative character of reality. There is no logical connection between these three themes in Renouvier's thought, but they are sustained by a belief in man's moral destiny. Renouvier did not, like Comte, regard mankind as taking precedence—for him, the individual was the primary reality. The finiteness of the individual can only be respected in a finite reality and there can be no question of real individuality unless there is freedom. This individuality (the person) is the highest category and is assumed for all other knowledge. The person means *conscience* (thus conscience and consciousness) and everything else is 'representation', as the relationship between subject and object, for the person. Thus the three basic themes are connected with a belief in the self-realization of the individual man. These themes are not connected with each other, but each supports this belief that is above all characteristic of Renouvier's thought, in which theory and practice, knowledge and will are never separated. In addition, Renouvier regarded his theses of finiteness and relativity as purely rational theses. He believed that the reality of the infinite was incompatible with the principle of contradiction. He gave no proofs for the relativity of reality, which he regarded as self-evident.

God is not an absolute and has no independent identity, but is rather the moral order, the demand of justice as such. This moral order is an order for the world and there is consequently no point in speaking about a God unless this is done in connection with the world. The demand of justice is not, however, automatically fulfilled in the world. Justice is always being violated by the egoism of the passions. This means that mankind lives in a constant 'state of war', in which one man lays snares for another. This is the darker side of free will which, on the other hand, also sustains everything that man builds up in the way of morality, art and science. History is a constant battle between these two opposite tendencies of the free will. Human history does not necessarily imply progress—everything depends on the attitude that every individual accepts as his own. Progress is therefore not a question of fate—it is a human affair.

In justifying his theme of freedom, Renouvier owed much to the man with whom he was friendly as a youth, JULES LEQUIER (1814-62). Lequier wrote very little and nothing was published until long after his death. His works are, however, now beginning to have a growing influence. Lequier strove tenaciously to escape from determinism at a time when it was the predominant characteristic of philosophy. The determinists could not comprehend freedom because they conceived everything according to the model of things. Lequier, however, did not regard the spiritualistic proof of freedom derived from inward experience as valid. For him, freedom was the necessary condition for the search for truth and it was found in this search as the necessary condition, that is, as the means by which we attain knowledge. Freedom is my ability to control and regulate my thoughts. Thus, the search for truth, as the act of my freedom, is at the same time the assertion of my freedom. Lequier opposed Hegel in that, unlike Hegel, he believed that man was not concerned with becoming, but with action and with forming himself—'doing, not becoming, but doing and, in doing, making oneself'.

ALPHONSE GRATRY (1805-72) went back to the tradition of Malebranche. His chief works were *De la connaissance de Dieu* (1853) and *De la connaissance de l'âme* (1858). Like Augustine, Pascal, Malebranche and Maine de Biran, writers to whom he frequently referred, Gratry was preoccupied with the question of the knowledge of God and of the soul. He was resolutely opposed to Hegel and to his deductive method and advocated the inductive mode of thought, by means of which the Infinite could be reached from the finite. He took as his point of departure human consciousness that was, in his view, characterized, on the one hand, by man's realization of his own insufficiency and, on the other, by his endeavour to transcend himself. It was on the basis of the structure of man's consciousness that Gratry believed that man had to establish with certainty the existence of God.

FÉLIX RAVAISSON (1813-1900) attended lectures by Schelling at Munich and was strongly influenced by the German philosopher, but his thought was above all akin to that of Maine de Biran. Ravaisson's point of departure was the idea that the mind has of an existence that coincides with its own activity and on which all other existence depends. For Ravaisson, this existence was not thought, as in the case of Descartes, whose dualism Ravaisson did not accept, but life. Life is the unity of mind and matter. The human consciousness presupposes a distance between setting oneself an aim and accomplishing it, a distance which is overcome by reflection. Habit, however, makes this distance less and less until it ultimately disappears. Habit is certainly an act of the intellect, but it is an unconscious act. This 'obscure insight' is a 'real intuition' in which the division between the real and the ideal, between being and thought, ceases to exist. Mind and nature thus coincide and nature displays the true character of its aspiration, in which necessity is only the interpretation of freedom. As Biran demonstrated, the soul reveals itself to thought as will and effort. But the will is always directed towards something and that something is good. The will's orientation towards and union with good is love, which is the essence of the soul. Ultimately, good is the Absolute, in other words, God. We reach God by an intuition of the whole of our person and God is Person. From this vantage point, we learn to see nature as a universal harmony, which speaks to us most clearly in the pure work of art, that can often reveal more truth to us than an entire philosophical treatise.

The thought of JULES LACHELIER (1832-1918) was in many respects a continuation of that of Ravaisson and, like his predecessor, Lachelier was also inspired by Maine de Biran. He was, however, less influenced by Schelling than by Kant. As he published very little himself, it is only possible to acquire a full understanding of his thought through the work of his disciples. Lachelier was opposed both to empiricism, which only acknowledges facts, but not their interconnection, and to eclecticism, in which thought and reality are separated by a gulf that cannot be bridged. In contrast, he proposed that reality is only in thought itself. The principle of causality alone is not sufficient to explain reality; in fact, the principle of finality is equally important. The principle of causality leaves us on the level of the abstract, the general and the mechanical. The principle of finality, on the other hand, confronts us with the concrete, the individual and the living. Thought is not simply a reflection of an objective world, but a movement towards good, the fullness of being. The laws of thought and those of being are identical. The idea of being or of truth proposes and affirms itself even if it is denied, when in fact an affirmation is made that it is true that it does not exist. Thought thus affirms itself and being in a first reflection. In a second reflection, it recognizes the diversity that is present in the inner and the outer world and, in a third reflection, it returns to itself as the source of being. Thought then shows itself as sovereign freedom which is conscious of itself. Nature, to which this free consciousness is bound, is overcome by the consciousness in reflection. Thought is therefore not subject to necessity, but is freedom realizing itself. Reflection is not a necessary movement, but is accomplished in freedom. Whoever does not accomplish it, remains in bondage. The absolute aspiration that is characteristic of freedom cannot stop short at formal thought, as its goal is not the idea of God, but God himself. The aspiring character of thought therefore goes beyond an immanent idealism towards a transcendent idealism.

JULES LAGNEAU (1851-94), one of Lachelier's disciples, never published anything during his lifetime. His influence continued to be felt in the work of his disciples and was extended by their posthumous publication of many of his writings. There are, he said, two degrees of freedom. The first degree consists in knowing the laws of nature, by which we set ourselves as reason against nature. Reason and nature are thus opposed to each other as two different factors. As reason, the ego dissociates itself from nature, but pays for this independence with its downfall. The ego must then choose between being and non-being. If it chooses non-being, it will remain in opposition to nature. If, on the other hand, it chooses being, it will subject itself to the value of absolute thought. In this absolute thought that thinks in us, the ego transcends itself and the opposition between reason and nature is overcome. Nature is no longer an abstraction and reason loses its independence which, in essence, is impotence. This union of the ego in absolute thought is only obtained in moral action. But moral action is the basis of philosophical thought. Recognizing the value of this is in itself a moral action. In the same way, recognizing God is also a moral action and this does not mean that it is not a reasonable action, but, on the contrary, implies that it is rational. The basis of the proof of the existence of God is our recognition of the value of thought. We reach certainty in this decision, but this certainty is not a state, but an act that we must be constantly renewing and deepening. This does not mean that every human being is enclosed within his own certainty—on the contrary, it is only through their universal nature that men understand each other. Thought, as man's capacity to transcend himself, is at the same time his capacity to discover others.

After the heyday of late scholasticism in the sixteenth century, scholastic thought was almost completely neglected throughout the eighteenth century. It occupied the attention of a number of men in religious orders, but did not find its way outside these monasteries. In this way, it also became more and more cut off from modern thought. The struggle over the relationship between faith and reason and over the foundations of morality, however, led certain Catholic scholars to turn their attention to scholasticism. The neo-scholastic movement was introduced mainly by Italian and German thinkers. In France, the development was later and took longer.

The growth of neo-scholasticism in the nineteenth century was actively encouraged by Pope Leo XIII who strongly recommended the study of scholasticism, and especially the philosophy of Thomas Aquinas, in his encyclical *Aeterni Patris* of 1879. Leo pointed out that the study of scholasticism should not lead those who were engaged in it to cut themselves off from modern thought and insisted that they should maintain contact with modern science and philosophy. In addition, Leo provided the impetus for the great critical edition of the works of Aquinas and for the establishment of a special chair in Thomism at the University of Louvain.

The institution of this chair and its occupation by Désire Mercier (1851-1926) in 1882 marked the beginning of a new period in neo-scholasticism. Mercier's philosophical activity resulted in the publication of his *Cours de philosophie,* a work planned on a broad basis (1884-94), and many smaller works in which he dealt with various problems raised by the natural sciences, biology and psychology. Mercier refused to have anything to do with a scholasticism that simply went back to the thirteenth century. His aim was to create a neo-scholasticism that was concerned with contemporary questions and was in vital contact with modern science and philosophy. His neo-scholasticism had to be an entirely independent science, independent even of theology.

Mercier derived his basic ideas from Aquinas, but he brought an independent mind to bear on them and extended them. In contrast to idealism, he defended the value of knowledge as reality. The concept of being was, for him, the most important philosophical concept. At the same time, he also discussed the concepts of existence and essence on the one hand, and on the other, those of unity, truth and goodness. A being can be either a substance or an accident. Substance is not a substratum for accidents, but a being that can exist in itself. An accident, on the other hand, can only exist in a substance. Mercier investigated particularly the quality and relations of accidents. Finally, he demonstrated how an analysis of the structure of beings can confront us more and more clearly with the question of an ultimate ground, our thought thus leading us, via beings, to the Being, God.

3. *English Philosophy*

Hume's criticism and Reid's appeal to common sense caused English thought to stagnate to some extent at the end of the eighteenth and the beginning of the nineteenth centuries. When this period of stagnation was overcome, English philosophy revived, but it retained its distinctive character—an empirical attitude towards reality and a strong tendency to regard all problems from a practical point of view.

This is very apparent in the thought of JEREMY BENTHAM

(1748-1832), whose most important work was *An Introduction to the Principles of Morals and Legislation* (1789). Bentham was above all interested in ethics. He looked for a basis for a moral doctrine that would not depend on arbitrary opinions and found it in two phenomena that were indisputable and accessible to everyone—pain and pleasure. The ethical task was to avoid pain and come to pleasure. For Bentham, the principle of morality was 'utility'—everything that avoided pain and achieved pleasure was utilitarian, only that which combated pain and gave pleasure was good and everything that gave pain and caused a loss of pleasure was bad. The morality of an action could therefore only be judged by experience, with the result that morality and utility were the same.

Bentham's ethics did not aim very high, but his teaching had the great merit of setting philosophy in motion again in England by stating a clear point of view. It is, moreover, not so flat as it appears at first sight. This is borne out by the influence of Bentham's teaching on a wide circle of political and social reformers. This influence was also undoubtedly due to the altruistic character of Bentham's utilitarianism, however difficult it may be to reconcile this with his basic idea of pain and pleasure. But the avoidance of pain and the achievement of pleasure was not, in Bentham's view, to be aimed at only for one's own sake, but for the sake of the greatest possible number of people—'the greatest happiness of the greatest number'.

JAMES MILL (1773-1836), whose most important work was his *Analysis of the Phenomena of the Human Mind* (1829), was concerned with the psychology that formed the most suitable basis for utilitarianism—association psychology, the psychology of the association of ideas. Man acts according to ideas (points of consciousness) which are combined in series according to definite laws. It is therefore a question of achieving the correct combination of ideas, so as to behave in the most utilitarian way possible. Utilitarianism thus became the strongest philosophical stream in English thought, despite the resistance of the poet COLERIDGE and the writer CARLYLE, whose basic philosophical ideas were strongly influenced by German romanticism and idealism.

James's son, JOHN STUART MILL (1806-73), was not un-affected by their criticism and it had the effect of making him think more deeply. All the same, he continued the utilitarian tradition in broad outline. He had a very open mind and did not avoid criticism, but tried to take advantage of it, believing that philosophy could only come about in honest open dialogue. His views on ethics and logic were especially important.

For him, ethics was not a science, but an art like aesthetics and politics. Every art, he believed, had aims, the desirability of which was apparent from experience. It was, moreover, possible to arrange these aims under a highest principle. As far as ethics was concerned, this highest principle was, in James Stuart Mill's opinion, the promotion of one's own and others' happiness. He realized that one's own happiness was inseparable from that of others and consequently gave great emphasis to the social character of ethics. Not only this, but also his recognition of aesthetic and intellectual pleasure clearly distinguished James Stuart Mill's utilitarianism from any one-sided ethics of pure pleasure. In psychology, he remained close to his father's ideas.

His logic was at the same time a theory of knowing. The only source of all knowledge is experience and the only correct scientific method is consequently the inductive method. All general judgements are simply abbreviated formulations for a quantity of separate experiences. The only law that is universally valid is the principle of causality, which James Stuart Mill defined as the firm and unconditional bond between two phenomena, so that the first phenomenon cannot appear without the second following. He went on to state four methods by which this connection could be established. In the last resort, logic could, in his opinion, be traced back to psychology, as logical relationships were in fact simply associations of ideas.

Darwin's theory of evolution exerted an enormous influence. CHARLES DARWIN (1809-82), whose major works were *Origin of Species* (1859) and *The Descent of Man* (1871), saw the entire organic world as a development from lower to higher forms, man being, at least for the present, the highest product of evolution and evolution itself being entirely governed by purely mechanical laws. Just as, in the world of plants and animals, only the most successful species remain in existence (the survival of the fittest), so too is the 'struggle for life' the highest law of life. Darwin put his theory forward simply as a hypothesis for the explanation of phenomena, but it became an absolute certainty for THOMAS HUXLEY (1825-95), who called Darwin's conscious abstention from metaphysical problems the first 'agnosticism'.

Independently of Darwin, HERBERT SPENCER (1820-1903) made the idea of evolution the basis of a comprehensive philosophical system, his *System of Synthetic Philosophy* (1860-96). Becoming, not being is knowable. Science proceeds from a few *a priori* truths—the indestructibility of matter, the perpetuity of movement and the law of the conservation of force. The whole process of the world consists of a continuous regrouping of matter and movement. Evolution is the transition to closer connection in matter ('integration') which is of necessity accompanied by a 'dissipation' of movement. In this way, the complicated has its origin in the simple—life has its origin in dead matter and man in organic nature. Evolution explains the mutual relationship of phenomena, but it does not explain why there are phenomena. The knowable world thus points to the unknowable—behind the world lies a great mystery, of which we know absolutely nothing (the great unknowable).

In his ethics, Spencer set utilitarianism within the framework of the evolutionary idea. Man is constantly learning how to adapt himself better and better to circumstances. An action is therefore morally good if it is adapted to environment, in other words, if it contributes to the happiness of the subject himself and to that of his descendants and his fellow-men. As a part of the process of evolution, this adaptation has a constantly changing content, with the consequence that the moral law itself is also constantly developing. By inheriting his ability to adapt from his ancestors, man has a spontaneous understanding of what is morally good and what is morally bad. Within the English-speaking world and even far beyond it, Spencer long exerted a powerful influence.

English philosophy had for some time been considerably influenced by German idealism, as we have seen. The publication of a book by JOHN HUTCHISON STIRLING (1820-1909), however, *The Secret of Hegel* (1865), led to a new development in English thought. The ideas expressed by Stirling in this book were quickly seized upon by others and neo-Hegelianism became the predominant philosophy in England at the turn of the century. English idealism reached its final development in a number of younger philosophers whose activity extended into the first quarter of the twentieth century.

JOHN HENRY NEWMAN (1801-90) occupied a very special place in English philosophy. Although he followed the empirical and practical tradition of English philosophy, Newman was principally concerned with the inward aspect of man. His theory of knowledge was above all a consideration of the correct mode of human knowledge and his ethics were ethics of the human conscience. His most important work was in the field of theology. After having played a leading part in the Anglican revival at the beginning of the nineteenth century, he became a Catholic in 1845. His theological ideas were sharply attacked by the Anglicans and aroused only moderate interest in the English Catholic Church. In 1879, however, he was created cardinal by Pope Leo XIII. Partly because his philosophical thinking was generally presented within the framework of the theological works, his significance as a philosopher has only very gradually come to be realized. For an understanding of his philosophy, his most important works are his *Essay on the Development of Christian Doctrine* (1845), *The Idea of a University* (1852), *Apologia pro Vita Sua* (1864) and *The Grammar of Assent* (1870).

Newman was opposed to the subordination of science to utility. The aim of science is science itself, because it corresponds to the highest claims of the human mind. Science may be indispensable in the carrying out of a profession, but it provides man with much more than he strictly needs simply in order to practise his profession. It extends and fortifies the mind and gives man a wide and balanced judgement. It is therefore much more than simply scholarship—it is an attitude of mind. Every science has points of contact with every other science and this is something that every scientist is required to understand. If he realizes this, he will be humble, because all insight into what is known is accompanied by an insight into what is not known. In every science there are assumptions about which the specialist in that science does not himself reflect. These assumptions are of a philosophical nature. Philosophy is therefore a synthetic science which gives us a deeper insight into the whole of reality. But it is precisely in this whole of reality that the problem of the existence of God is posed. Here we are on the frontier between philosophy and theology, where philosophy points beyond its own frontiers to theology. Theology is therefore indispensable to the entirety of the sciences, because, if it is absent, the other sciences, which are incapable of fulfilling its special function, assume its task, with consequent confusion in all the fields of science.

Newman set out his view of the meaning of science, as outlined above, in *The Idea of a University*. His ideas about human thought in concrete were formulated above all in his *Grammar of Assent*, a book which he wrote to demonstrate the rational nature of the act of faith. His argument, however, presupposes a consideration of the human mode of thought as such and it is this that is of importance to philosophy. Newman above all made a clear distinction between purely 'notional' assent and 'real' assent. A notional assent is purely rational consent to the correctness of a statement. A real assent, on the other hand, is the acknowledgement of a statement with the whole of one's being, intellect, will and heart. A recognition of this kind takes hold of man in his personal being and transforms him. Newman thus showed that man could recognize the existence of God either notionally, in which case his assent would not bear fruit, or really, in which case his assent would affect him in the depths of his being.

Newman then went on to set out the difference between 'assent' and 'inference'. Formal inference is always concerned with a series of judgements, assent with the recognition of one judgement. Assent of this kind usually comes about in a very complicated manner. Feeling and will play a part in it, but this does not mean that the assent thereby becomes irrational. In day-to-day existence, thought always works as a component of the whole human personality. Feeling and will may mislead thought, which is a component in every action, but they can also support it. That is why the insight that is important to life does not, in the first place, come from formally correct inference, but from the correct orientation of the whole human person as such. When the whole man has a pure disposition, his implicit thought leads him to the correct insight. This

H

ability to attain a correct insight without formal and logical reasoning was what Newman called the 'illative sense', because it did not work along the indirect path of a direct inference, but by means of 'illation'. He also showed how man's vital decisions were made in this way—that they were, in other words, the result of the purity of man's disposition, and that his religious attitude had its point of departure in his illative sense, which at the same time justified his religious attitude.

It is clear that Newman assigned a very important part to conscience in his study of concrete thought. He regarded conscience as the implicit insight that gives direction to all our actions, including our thinking. For Newman, the conscience was the most personal element in man, in a sense the point at which thought, will and heart converged, the highly personal moment at which man transcended himself and recognized God. The human conscience was, for him, the voice of God in us. Newman offered it as the most clear proof of the existence of God.

Newman's influence was restricted in his own age, but it increased rapidly after his death. He is now regarded as one of the nineteenth-century thinkers who foresaw the problems of the twentieth century.

INDEX

INDEX